The Life
of
Halime Gulsu

The Heavenly Teacher
Murdered in Prison

Written by

Zeynep Kayadelen

Edited by

Hafza Girdap

The Life of Halime Gulsu

The Heavenly Teacher
Murdered in Prison

www.silencedturkey.org

Published: November 2022
ISBN: 9798365685956

CONTENTS

ABOUT THE HIZMET MOVEMENT

Hizmet is a transnational civil society initiative that advocates for the ideals of human rights, equal opportunity, democracy, non-violence, and the emphatic acceptance of religious and cultural diversity. This widespread movement began in Turkey as a grassroots community in the 1970s in the context of social challenges being faced at the time: violent conflicts among ideologically and politically driven youth, desperate economic conditions, and decades of a state-imposed ideology of discrimination that mandated a particular lifestyle.

Over the years, Hizmet has transformed from a grassroots community in Turkey to a much wider global effort with participants from all walks of life. Their work is centered upon promoting philanthropy and community service, investing in education to cultivate virtuous individuals, organizing intercultural and interfaith dialogue events to promote a peaceful coexistence.

Hizmet participants are inspired by the ideas and example of Fethullah Gulen, a Muslim scholar who has expressed the belief that serving fellow humans is as serving God.

For more information: www.afsv.org

EDITOR'S NOTE

Advocates of Silenced Turkey (AST) is a non-governmental organization that runs its activities on a voluntary basis since 2018. The aim of AST is to bring before international public opinion the human rights violations including torture and the unlawful court trials and proceedings, which have been encountered in Turkey especially the last ten years. After 2016, more than 160,000 innocent people lost their jobs in both public and private sectors, with accusations and unjust convictions of being connected with the coup attempt. The state of emergency, which was announced on July 20, 2016, gave the government unchecked powers - in the disguise of combatting terrorism - to persecute thousands of people with no accountability and to undermine the fundamental principles of a democratic society and the most basic principles of universal human rights and values such as freedom of expression and freedom of the press. Today, tens of thousands of highly qualified professionals such as judges, prosecutors, doctors, teachers, journalists, academics, and military officers have been detained and imprisoned in Turkey due to bogus terrorism charges. Around 5,000 of them are women, along with nearly 345 children who stay with their mothers in prisons. Hundreds of thousands of people have little or no hope of surviving the grueling atmosphere in Turkey, and as they are banned from leaving the country, they have no other choice but to flee at the risk of losing their lives by crossing the borders via dangerous routes. Some of them have not survived this difficult journey.

As the Advocates of Silenced Turkey, we engage in a number of activities in order not to keep silent about the injustices that have been taking place in Turkey where the rule of law has been suspended for a long time.

APH (Archiving the Persecution of Hizmet) project of recording and archiving the testimonies of victims, aims to shed light on the injustices suffered by thousands of people in Turkey. Our volunteers have conducted hundreds of interviews and thanks to their efforts, the victimizations, and hardships that the victims experienced are now being recorded in both spoken and written formats. The main purpose of this project is to ensure that these tragic stories are not allowed to fade into oblivion but are rather recorded accurately and impartially to leave firsthand sources for future generations. We also aim to bring this persecution to the attention of academics, media organizations, human rights associations, prominent community leaders, and government representatives at the international level.

"The Life of Halime Gulsu" is the product of a long-term endeavor. We would like to thank everyone who made tireless and valuable contributions to this work. We wish that Turkey will soon transform into a democratic society in which fundamental values like universal human rights and the rule of law are duly observed.

We dedicate this work, which is based on true stories…
…to the thousands of people in Turkey, who have been
deprived of their liberty and still face persecution.
…to innocent people who had to flee their homeland
and get separated from their families.
…to all victims who have set out for a new life in which
they just want to live freely without any further injustice.
…and to those who have lost all their hope of going
back and living in their homelands.

We sincerely thank…
Our author Zeynep Kayadelen
Book Editor Hafza Girdap
Translator E.Y.
English Editors Barbara W., Hande Hur
Illustrator Ummu Korku
Cover Design Muhsin Nazif
…and everyone else who contributed to this project.

PREFACE

WE HAVE DIED MANY TIMES

They believed a lie at the first chance they got…

And defamed you, me, and many like us

But we were only children, so pure, rolling in sweet dreams…

Unaware of how evil could evil get

If we only knew that the darkness would fall so deep…

Those sunny days would be so far away…

The cheerful, radiant, friendly voices of yesterdays would be but an echo

We are dead now

Your plots took our lives away from us

Thrown around by surprise, we are torn down

Wouldn't know who killed whom and why, while filling up the graves

Like little children growing up in a day…

We stared after everything we lost

No one heard us when we just whispered…

I'm only a child…I belong to here…please don't do this!

They lined up to throw the biggest stones at us…

In front were our relatives, our brothers, our friends.

We have died many times
You would not believe, you would doubt…
But we have countless graves in the Anatolian steppes
In the sunny Mediterranean, in the lavender scented
Aegean.
When our hearts were broken into million pieces…
So did our love in our hearts, for our homeland and our
nation
We have died many times and set off on the roads…
Survived evil ambushes…
Walked away barefoot from every memory we had saved
We have died from your hands
Some of us took refuge in the shadows of other flags
New and friendly winds wiped the tears from our eyes
And now, you don't need to come after us or bring us
back
We are dead to you, we bloomed elsewhere
Some of us joined to our Lord
The rest of us surrounded the world like verbenas, roses,
and hyacinths
One day, your captives, too, will be set free from your
bloody cage
Even though they are in the dungeons, they are with us…
Far far away from you

O you with evil spirits, do understand this…

We are dead now!

Don't touch our corpses with your bloody hands…

Put those bloody hands on your own faces

Stay in dark and in evil…

Alone with your heart devoid of mercy

***

This poem is dedicated…

…to the people who were subjected to genocide in recent years recently in Turkey.

…to those innocent people who lost their lives because they could not cope with the evil that reached unprecedented heights.

…to those who were mercilessly killed for reasons which were but absurd and outrageous.

There is a quote attributed to Albert Einstein: "According to idiots, people are divided into categories like race, gender, nationality, age, status, color, religion, and language. However, it is not that complicated. **People are only divided into two: good people and evil people.**" This saying is so true. There are two simple truths that should never be forgotten. Good and evil. Evil never gives up. Although humanity advances in science and technology, primitivity and monstrosity remain current. Humanity can never be cleansed from fascism. In fact, sometimes the stage is entirely left to the fascists. The blood spilled by the thugs who utter big words paints the streets red. The murderers skillfully hide behind some noble virtues and drive the society into a frenzy. People attack left and right like a drunk who will be ashamed of what he has done when he wakes up. The so-called coup of July 15, 2016 was exactly the starting point of such a frenzy. Turkey was ruled by a dictator who was an expert in managing the darkness, grudge and hatred that accumulated in the souls of the people. They accused the Hizmet volunteers of coup plotters and started a terrible witch hunt. The rule of law gave way to revenge. Not only those who had an account in a specific bank or who were subscribed to a specific newspaper, but even their relatives were imprisoned. One day, when the Turkish people come to their senses from this insanity, I am sure they will be filled with shame... And they will ask for forgiveness.

But that day will never come for those who were killed like Halime. She will be waiting for her murderers in the Divine Presence of God. Had Halime and angel-hearted people like her lived, they could have forgiven their murderers. Because they were good people with compassion in their hearts for everyone. I would like to call out to her if I could and say the following:

No Halime, never forgive them! They didn't kill only you. They destroyed the values of Islam, the religion of love and peace. They killed the spirits and the beliefs.

Never forgive those who plot against love and tolerance! Because you lived your life in the direction of love and tolerance. You lived for these values.

Dear Halime, you were a true hero. You were killed for taking care of children whose parents were imprisoned.

May the love and mercy you put on glorify your soul and give you wings upon the slopes of the Heaven…

May your soul rest in peace…

The Life
of
Halime Gulsu

The Heavenly Teacher

Murdered in Prison

O you wretched ones! Know that at the end of the road, each and every evil deed you commit will surely be waiting for your arrival!

Here we are, in a hospital room. The monotone buzz of the long white fluorescent lights scratches away at the cold, hard walls. Drops of blood are splattered on the dirty gray tiles on the floor, and the open trash bin in the corner looks like it's about to spill over its gruesome contents. The lifeless body lying on the gurney, fading away on a heap of wrinkled bed sheets, that's me. As the caretakers shut off the machines surrounding my lifeless body one by one, they complain about how little the raise on their salaries had been. How strangely accustomed they have become to the cold, hard reality of death; one yawns and stretches as though he's merely pulling down the shutters to his shop for the night. What a blessing it is that I am finally far, far away from everything now. My heart, broken into a thousand pieces, has finally found some peace. My soul took wing and flew high like a bird broken free from its cage. It soared on to a horizon where no vulgar hand would be able to reach it anymore...

Minutes later, a black body bag was brought in, and my body was placed inside, the body that I hope will give me its blessing. I tried my best to be gentle towards it while I was alive. I did all I could to take good care of it; that is, up until the day I somehow crossed paths with those evil souls. Once I had fallen prisoner to those tyrants, sadly, taking good care of my body became an impossibility.

Here they go, closing up the zipper to the body bag. Do I even care? My black-and-blue lips are clamped together like I have no more words left in me to cry out to those tyrants. A last smile, frozen on my ghostly white face. It won't be long now until they take away my body into a morgue and tuck it neatly into an ice-cold cabinet. No harm done, I'm not there anymore. It makes no difference that my body is lying there, naked, in a plastic bag, on an ice-cold metal tray. I'm not cold anymore.

I will be waiting patiently in the morgue with the other dead bodies, waiting until a family member comes to take me away. Come to think of it, the only family member who would actually be able to come fetch me is my middle older brother. Oppression and persecution had scattered the rest of my family far, far away. It will be my dear brother carrying my green-veiled coffin with tears in his eyes. I wish nobody would cry. I've never wanted to upset anyone; they all know this. But what can we do? Nothing stands in the way of the will of the Almighty! How I wish there would be a scarf bursting with the scent of my dear mother to spread over my coffin, my dear mother who I never had a chance to say goodbye to... Goodbye to you o world... farewell to you o tyrants... At last, I'm free... I know the animosity you carry in your hearts; you might as well claim that I am only deceiving you, playing dead. Oh, how you would have taken pleasure in killing me, not once but many many times, over and over again. Let your dark world eat away at you! Your morgue-like hearts devoid of the warmth of love and compassion is all the punishment you will ever need!

My name is Halime Gülsu. I was killed. I am the victim of a sneaky and heartless murder. My murderers watched with their watering mouths as I melted away like a candle. Meanwhile, they kept building their sultanate; a sultanate steadily rising over the pain and sorrow of myself and others like me. But alas! They do not know! They do not know that no matter how magnificent their sultanate may be, in the end it will surely be trifling, transient and nothing more!

O death... The mysterious gateway to the worlds unknown... Dear "death", you are the one that everyone fears the most, the one that everyone is most curious about, yet still the one that everyone chooses to live as though you don't exist... Now, at the age of thirty-three, I have the pleasure to make your acquaintance. There were so many things that I still wanted to do and experience in this world; but they didn't let me. Those who locked me up in a dark and dingy dungeon, tossed aside like a useless piece of trash, may they never see the light of day themselves! My final moments in this world were of a spring night where colors and scents rained down in droves... I closed my eyes to this life like the gentle closing of the petals of an evening flower. As I lay here in my grass-covered grave, far away from my murderers, I wait for the coming of the Judgment Day...

You may be wondering: why do I bother to tell you my mournful story that ultimately ended with a pile of dirt? Because I, too, wanted to cry out about how unnecessary and foolish it is to run after evil in this world which is filled with the monumental truth of death! Yes, death ultimately leaves all the things that people turn on each other's throats for, a senseless and meaningless heap. And to those who had their share in the pain and suffering I went through, I want to shout out to their faces, "O you wretched ones, know that at the end of the road, each and every evil deed you commit will surely be waiting for your arrival!"

I came into this world in the village of Tarsus Pirömerli in October of 1984. I was born into a beautiful family. Being the youngest of four siblings, not to mention the only daughter, was nothing to complain about. My father was the imam of the local mosque, and my mother was a homemaker. The village I grew up in was like any other Anatolian village, full of poverty. And like any other Anatolian villager, we did the best we could to stand on our own feet with whatever means we had. With no running water inside the house, we would fetch water from afar on donkeys. Since early childhood, I helped my mother at home with daily household chores. All hardships aside, I loved living out in the country. What child would be unhappy living out in the middle of nature? They say that from the time I was very little there was always a calmness about me, and I could get along with just about anyone. Who knows, maybe it was because I sensed I didn't have much time in this world, and I didn't want to waste time and energy with unnecessary bickering. Those were the days when my only worry was falling down and scratching a knee... Oh the sweet days of childhood, those wonderful days that passed like a dream... Days when we lived happily with no worries, when we were oblivious to the evils that lurked in dark corners, oblivious to evil men who conjured up evil plans to harm others... My days were spent playing with friends, strolling about in the sweet and innocent valleys of childhood. One thing that was different about me -- as told by my mother -- was that when I was little, I had an interesting habit of eating soil. Later I searched about why some people eat dirt. Well, apparently it was kind of related to certain deficiencies in a person's blood. So, I'm guessing that my illness had been born with me when I came into this world. Kind of like birth and death are born together...

We lived in that same village until 2002, though I myself had moved out of my parent's home prior to that date - right after I finished elementary school, to continue my education. I started to attend the Religious Vocational Middle School, and all seemed well; however, it was not. I was nowhere near as strong or energetic as my peers. I would get sick often and had a weak appetite. They said it was because of anemia. From the outside, I looked completely normal, but from the inside, something was wrong. Thus began our tiresome journey through the four corners of the city of Malatya, rushing from one doctor to the other, hoping to find a reason for my deteriorating health. Temporary solutions and supplements with no diagnosis provided no cure, no relief. Friends and family were also eager to provide expertise and recommendations about this food and that herb, certain that all would be well if only I followed their prescribed diet. I found myself in a pool of curative concoctions, different types of honeys, and syrups of all sorts, yet I was still no better.

As the days rolled by with its ups and downs, my educational adventure continued at a high school in the city of Mersin. Because my family was still living back home in our small village, accommodation was still an issue for me. Still, I did not give up. I was able to complete my high school education seesawing between staying with relatives and living in the dormitory. As I had grown and matured, my illness got more serious and chronic. On the day of my graduation from high school, my health came crashing down. I had fainted, lost consciousness and was in a coma. When the doctors at the public hospital had lost all hope for me, I was sent to the university hospital. Thankfully, a doctor there was truly an expert in his field and made the right diagnosis for my illness. They had promptly started my treatment, and I had been brought back to life, so to speak. Long story short, my dear illness and I had finally been formally acquainted... I was officially a Systemic Lupus Erythematosus (SLE) patient. This was a rare type of blood disease that had a pretty sneaky way of taking over the body. The treatment process was certainly not an easy one. There was quite a long list of medicines that I needed to take, not to mention that this was a chronic disease which required me to be under constant monitoring.

It certainly was not easy for me to acknowledge and accept a disease which was considered 100% incurable. Though it had been disheartening at first, with time I guess I adapted and learned to live with it. I said to myself, "This was sent to me from my Lord, Allah Almighty." I would do my best to get along with the good old Lupus. Since we were to be together till death do us part, it would learn to put up with me just as I would learn to put up with it. Besides, wasn't life itself ultimately fatal in the end anyway? I certainly was not of a nature to hide under a blanket and complain that I was "so sick." For one thing, I had my education to complete. I had dreams and aspirations; I had hopes for the future. I had to get stronger, feel better, and become a teacher one day. When I was feeling well and strong, I was attending a teaching institution to prepare for the university admission exams. I was trying to do my best to hold on to life and "suck the marrow out of it!"

Systemic Lupus is a fatal disease, a terminal illness. It entails a troubling type of treatment in which the prescribed medicine also functions in suppressing the body's own immune system. In other words, while trying to dodge SLE on one hand, it was very likely that you could find yourself taken down by a much simpler disease. Anyone else in my place may very well have chosen to shy away from making any long-term plans, choosing to be taken care of in the peaceful atmosphere of their cozy home, rather than chasing after an education and a professional career. Whereas in my case, there was a fire burning ablaze inside me. I wanted to thrive, to succeed; I wanted to be useful. I wanted to contribute to the society that I was a part of. I must have been sent down to this world with a purpose, I simply could not leave it empty-handed. I studied theology for two years after high school, but this was not enough. I had to do more. And I did. After several attempts, I finally scored enough points in the university admission exams to be accepted into the university and department that I was aspiring to.

One should have a goal in life, a goal that will blossom like spring flowers into the heart with each new day...

2011 was the year when I started to study English Language and Literature at Gaziantep University. Nothing was standing between me and my dream of becoming a teacher anymore. I was excited and enthusiastic about this new chapter in my life. I'd always helped out with neighbor children when they needed help with schoolwork. In fact, it was through my tutoring sessions with them that the idea of becoming a teacher had blossomed within me. "You should definitely be a teacher," they would say as they smiled up at me. And here was my ticket, finally. I packed my suitcases and journeyed on to Antep. By that time, I had found a certain kind of harmony with my illness which I now considered an indispensable part of me. My treatments continued along with my studies at the university as I adjusted to a new life in the city of Antep.

Due to my father's work situation, after completing elementary school, I had continued with my education away from home. During my university years, I stayed in the dormitories and student homes that were affiliated with Hizmet movement. This movement was widely known for providing opportunity and support to children coming from families of limited means, and it had surely won appreciation in my heart as well. They touched the lives of so many poor children from different parts of Anatolia and provided guidance in preparing them for a better, brighter future. I found it both remarkable and commendable that they did not ask for any fees from the students who did not have the means to pay for the services they received. I saw firsthand just how selfless and giving the members of the Hizmet movement were.

I understood much better that it was not clothes, jewelry, money, or possessions that beautified a human being. True beauty lay in helping others, in striving to make the world a better place for all. And this should have been the ultimate purpose in life, the very reason that we had been sent to this world. To live with faith, with love, with compassion and grace... To make the effort to make someone smile... I had found my calling in life. I had found the purpose, the goal, the calling that would bring meaning to this short worldly life we live. Living a life in pursuit of a fancy house, beautiful clothes, and gourmet food alone would not suffice for a person of mind and heart. These wouldn't satisfy me, either. The answer to how I should be living my life lay in the answers to the questions "Where I had been sent here from?" and "Where I would be headed when I die?" And I had long since found my answers.

I was now a volunteer of the Hizmet¯movement. From fundraising programs and organizations, to tutoring poor students, I did my best to put in my share. Days came and went as I rushed from the classes in the college to my own students, friends, and chores waiting for me at home. Days were spent in a sweet string of events and busyness. After four years I graduated from the university. I started teaching at a private school in Antep, Gazikent High School. Entering the classroom every morning and being greeted with the youth, energy twinkling in their eyes… filled me with such excitement and happiness, beyond description. I was in love with my profession. I was training my students not only for a good professional life and a good future, but also to be good human beings. I was part of a faith system that taught me to love all human beings, regardless of whether I know them or not. That love was the focal point of my life, the sole light enlightening and guiding me on my path. And so, to nurture this love and keep it growing, to be worthy and deserving of this love, I ran and ran to all the people around me who needed a helping hand. Due to my illness, I was frequently thinking about death and what lay beyond it. So, I gave my best effort to live a life where I would not break anyone's heart or hurt anyone. This way or that, when I finally came to the end of the time I was given, I should not find myself in the middle of something that I would regret. Thank God, everything was going well. Even my illness was well under control now. Taking medicines regularly and most importantly being in a good state of mind and heart, the effect of the illness on my body was hardly noticeable anymore.

No matter the circumstances, one thing is always constant: time always runs its course and the flow stops for no one; it doesn't matter if you're tired, or sick, or whatever else. If, somehow, we can leave tiny little marks in the pages of history through our life story, how beautiful! As my own story was slowly weaving its course, a gust of wind had swept over my family home and taken my father with it. My beloved father's death in 2015 hit me deeply, and I was shaken with the feeling of how near death and the afterlife truly was. The giant of a man that I knew as my father had now become one with the earth, like a dry leaf fallen to the ground. Yet, what about his thoughts, his ideas, his memories? They couldn't have just blown into thin air and disappeared just like that. My mind and my heart agreed that he was not gone, he had just changed places. The afterlife was such a realm that you could not take anything worldly with you, not even your "own" body. Only your deeds... I was reminded then, once again, that this world was only good to serve as a good-deed savings deposit box.

With the death of my father, my older brothers felt more like fathers to me. Having three older brothers was nothing to complain about, if you ask me. They were all so full of compassion and affection towards me. Also, maybe because I was the only girl in our household, there was a very special bond between me and my mother. Especially after my father's passing, spending time with my mother, taking her out shopping was a grand pleasure for me. Naturally, this made it all the worse for my dear mother when I, too, passed on to the after-realm because she not only lost her daughter, but she also lost her best friend, her confidante.

Oh...the humans! They think they know everything... when, in fact, the first thing they should know should be their place in this universe. How weak and helpless we are... Just as we have no power over where and how we will be coming into this world, we have also no power over what we will encounter just a few steps later in this journey called life. Well, it turns out that, thinking you have control over everything and constantly making plans for the future could be described as - to say the least - being arrogant. And here I would like to add Hizmet movement members as well...yes, we, too, were leaving the best days of our lives behind as we headed into a dark future, though we did not know it then. Black clouds were gathering around and heading in our direction, though we did not anticipate it at the time. Our hearts were to be filled with broken dreams, bewilderment, confusion and fear, though we did not foresee it.

Why, you ask? How unfortunate that, just like me, my country was also suffering from a chronic disease that was pushing her towards an inevitable death with each passing minute. My dear country, wounded so many times, over and over, by conflicts like Alawis[1] vs. Sunnis[2], Turks vs. Kurds, etc. Injustice, widespread aggression and lynching had destroyed countless lives already. So many of us had believed that by now this poisonous disease had been taken under control and that the country was on its road to healing. Stability, the rising of the economy; they seemed to be on the right track. Democracy had finally settled in and found its place within the country in the recent years, and it seemed as though the country was finally starting to calm down and settle. There was a growing consciousness within society and no one would not turn a

---

1   Around 10-15% of the population living in Turkey is Alawis, who are following a belief system that incorporates aspects of Shi'a and Sunni Islam as well as the traditions of other and much older belief systems in the region.
2   Sunni Islam is by far the largest denomination of Islam, comprising around 85% of the Muslim population in the world. The term Sunni comes from the word *Sunnah*, which means the teachings, actions, and examples of the Prophet Muhammad (Peace be upon Him).

blind eye towards blindly targeting and lynching a part of society ever again; or so we had thought. We found out in an excruciatingly painful way that this was not the case at all! As biting as it is, I cannot leave it unsaid. The people whom I loved dearly as my fellow citizens, the people of my country whom I trusted so greatly, it all turned out to be nothing but a monumental disappointment, an indescribable heartache. In the aftermath of all that was experienced, I understood clear as day that the trusted common sense and judgment of the Anatolian people had been buried under a cloud of dust and rotted away with the historic memorabilia of a legendary past that was now only displayed in museums. The same Anatolian people I once knew and loved had, this time around, nurtured in its fearsome embrace a monstrosity so cruel and heartless that it would eventually destroy me, at age 33, in the prime of my lifetime, along with anyone else that it could get its claws on. Finally, when one night that monster finally jumped out of its cave and started pouncing on the innocent and the helpless, the only thing we could do was freeze in horror. Our tears flowed as one with the blood that was spilled in vain, our hands resting shakily on our aching hearts...

If it's the fox calling the adhan, better to keep an eye on the coop.

Azerbaijani Proverb

Every so often, my mind would wander back in history, thinking about the generations of believers that came before us and the pain and suffering they were put through on account of their beliefs. And then I would think about my own self. I would feel thankful to be living in a time where we had the freedom to live our lives in line with our faith, and we were not being lynched for it. Because we were civilized now; witch hunts were an outdated idea of the past and people could not be persecuted due to their ideas and beliefs, right? Alas! How terribly mistaken I had been! It turns out that the desire to destroy and wipe out had secretly been lurking in the hearts of some so-called humans, silently waiting for the right conditions and timing. Our bright and sunny days were about to come to an indefinite end. I use the word "our" because the planned genocide that was closing in on us had set its eyes on each and every member of the Hizmet movement. Why? The corruption investigations[3] of 2013

---

3 The December 17-25, 2013, corruption scandal in Turkey refers to a criminal investigation that involves several key people in the Turkish government. Prosecutors accused 14 people, including several family members of the cabinet ministers, the director of state-owned bank (Halkbank) and Turkish-Iranian businessman Reza Zarrab, of bribery,

that had been conducted against certain officials who were part of the ruling government of the time had very much upset the ruling government. The investigations had been blasted on all newspapers and media channels throughout the country. The government officials who had been caught red-handed with shoe boxes full of dirty money stashed in their homes started building up a grudge not only against the law enforcement authorities who exposed them but to anyone and everyone who may have (at their own discretion) the slightest relations with those authorities. Either the "thieves" would be given an apology, or they would be taking their revenge.

Needless to say, the honest and committed policemen who were merely doing their job did not apologize to a corrupt government. The media organs that were affiliated with the Hizmet movement were also against the corruption and fraudulent acts within the ruling government. Supporting a group of people who used religion to cover up their own mistakes and desires was clearly out of the question. Consequently, from that point on, the ruling government and its leading dictator

---

corruption, fraud, money laundering and gold smuggling. In March 2016, Reza Zarrab was arrested in Miami. In November 2017, Zarrab cooperated with federal prosecutors and has become key witness in the case of money laundering and violating sanctions on Iran.

Erdogan placed the Hizmet movement right in the middle of their dart board. Suddenly, bought-out newspapers and media channels had turned against us. With a devilish mentality and intelligence, they started manipulating the conservative and religious soft-spot of the society. They started spreading lies about the inspirational leader of the Hizmet movement, Fethullah Gulen[4], saying that he was in fact a Christian missionary, that he was a heathen. To the West, on the other hand, they said that he was an Islamist fundamentalist. They fabricated so-called evidence. What's more, they spread rumors abroad to countries with Hizmet-established schools that the Hizmet movement members were actually religious fundamentalists who should be extradited. Back home in Turkey, they spread rumors that these same people were in fact American, English, German, what have you, spies. They fabricated scenarios with fabricated names and fabricated plots. No matter how poorly fabricated the scenarios were, the Turkish society itself had eroded to such a point that they easily became pawns in whatever

---

4 Fethullah Gulen is an Islamic scholar, preacher and social advocate, whose decades-long commitment to education, altruistic community service, and interfaith harmony has inspired millions in Turkey and around the world. Described as one of the world's most important Muslim figures, Gulen has reinterpreted aspects of Islamic tradition to meet the needs of contemporary Muslims. He has dedicated his life to interfaith and intercultural dialogue, community service and providing access to quality education. For more information, please visit www.afsv.org

dirty scenario was played out for them.

Once the Turkish society had reached the desired conditions, the government started brewing up excuses to shut down and destroy any and all establishments--such as schools, dormitories, teaching institutions, etc.--that had been founded through the hard work of dedicated Hizmet volunteers. Like many of my friends and colleagues, I was shocked and heartbroken. In all its years of active service, not one child had ever received harm of any kind in any of these establishments. On the contrary, they had been given the best education and training in the country and had made their way to the best positions within society. Why, then, all this animosity? Why were these establishments, built using the donations of good people, being shut down in the blink of an eye? I thought long and hard to find an answer to these questions. Why do human beings do such evil things?

And, I think, I was slowly starting to understand how true evil came out into the open. I was seeing it happen right before my very eyes. One thing was for sure, nobody wakes up one morning and, all of a sudden, decides, "Oh, why don't I commit some evil today!" Besides, nobody ever describes themselves as evil. In fact, it's just the opposite. That journey usually starts with an "I'm the best." When a person is suffering from an illness of the heart, like envy, hatred, or excessive ambition, it eats away at you until eventually your conscience is decayed of all its light. And once that is paired up with some power and influence, then destruction follows close by, hidden behind excuses that even the perpetrator would find hard to believe. For instance, how tragicomical that you would claim to be healing someone by hurting them. I suppose this is the reason why there is so much pain and suffering in the world today. People with blood-stained hands and tongues were giving fine speeches of the greatest callings while, in reality, they were serving the darkness smothering their souls. Take a look at any genocide narrative and you will see it clearly: oppression and injustice wrapped in a glittery box of benevolence and lofty ideals. During that time, I came to understand, once more, that how you do the service is just as important as what you are doing the service for. If there was no room left for compassion and kindness in a person's soul, then all other qualities would inevitably lose all significance.

Government leaders, through defamation, lawlessness, thievery, and bribery, claimed they were doing service in the name of Islam. When children suffer for the sake of a "cause," when the rule of law is trampled upon and people are killed in the name of a calling -- that is nothing more than a manic excuse rather than a true calling or a cause. These monstrous individuals claiming to be the great defenders of the religion of Islam were in fact only stacking up their fortunes and skillfully deceiving the majority of the nation while they were at it. Given these circumstances, the Hizmet movement with its universal message that Islam is a religion of peace and love now stood on a completely opposite platform from this radical new front.

And now for that dark and gloomy night when all evil had reached its peak, the night of July 15 of 2016... It was a summer night; my mother and I had just finished our nightly prayers and were sitting together. It was a hot and humid summer evening, the kind that makes it almost hard to even breathe. There was a different kind of heaviness in the air. We were going about our regular routine-- a little bit of TV, then off to bed... All of a sudden, news of an attempted coup started blasting on the TV, and it felt as though time froze, sliced right through with a knife. My mom and I stood there gaping at each other, shocked. All TV stations were blasting the same images over and over.

What was this that I was hearing? Soldiers, weapons, coup d'état... it felt as though the words were being hammered into my brain. The leader of the ruling government, Erdogan, was calling on the people to take to the streets: "Go out into the streets and do whatever you need to save our country from occupation!" These were the words flowing from his mouth. Save the country? From whom? From its own soldiers? Wasn't this a bit odd? Shouldn't the proper advice be to keep peaceful and calm, to avoid any fighting and conflict, to avoid even the slightest chance of any bloodshed? Shouldn't the words have been, "Do not go out into the streets, stay calm, do not act on impulse," or something like that? A situation too murky to make out any kind of meaning terrified me to my core. Were there really armed citizens marching out on the streets now? Could this be the start of a civil war? Grief and anxiety took over me, I didn't know what to do with myself. My heart was beating in my chest like a bird thrashing about, looking for a way out. Feeling so helpless and so weak, I merely looked out the window into the street. Though quiet like its usual self, the city was not the same city it was just an hour ago. Had we, a whole country, all of a sudden, fallen into a black hole filled to the rim with evil and malice? What kind of a morning would we be waking up to the next day? I took refuge in God, the Lord of all the Worlds. What else could I do but turn to the Creator and pray until the morning light, pray that this commotion would settle down and that no blood would be spilled between citizens of the same country?

The speakers from the mosques blasted calls to

prayer and chants all through the night. What really had my heart trembling was how Erdogan announced right from the beginning that members of the Hizmet movement were responsible for the attempted coup and that they would be severely called to account. He called it a parallel state, an armed terrorist organization. How could they possibly know who was behind the coup when the soldiers actively carrying out the operation had not yet even been apprehended? There was something shady about it all. I even spoke to my dear mother about it that night. Let's say even if there was the possibility of certain individuals being misled or conned into being a part of such a scandal, there was no way in the world anyone could make me believe that Hizmet members had planned and executed this. They were accusing Hizmet of dark and murky acts whereas Hizmet has always been a source of light and life. Theirs were accusations of conflict and animosity whereas the core of the Hizmet movement lay in peace and the art of living together in harmony. This is the way it had always been for the past forty years. Weapons, politics, and extremism were never on the Hizmet agenda.

The night of July 15, 2016 was a long, long night. The morning after, our gracious Lord rose the sun to shine over us, but darkness lay ahead for my country and its people. I could see that same darkness in the eyes of my neighbors with whom I had carried on happy and light-hearted conversations just a day ago. They knew how closely I was involved in the Hizmet movement and started taunting me on how the real face of Fethullah Gulen had finally been exposed. I tried to express to them as best I could that Fethullah Gulen could not have approved of such an act, that they shouldn't go jumping to conclusions without knowing the whole truth.

What had just happened... in just a matter of a single night? The environment of peace and trust had been destroyed. People had taken to the streets and social media, in a crazed mode, swearing and belching out words of hatred and insults, shouting for revenge. In their eyes, Hizmet had been turned into a horrible monstrosity, and the people were all in agreement that anything associated with it deserved to be destroyed in cold blood. The circumstances showed that what we had witnessed the night before had merely been a spark, and that the fire was just getting started. This was a fire that had been deliberately set up to burn us, the people of Hizmet. My dear mother saw the tension in the air. She saw the anger and animosity people felt towards Hizmet, and she advised me not to get into any arguments with anyone around this very hot agenda. However, I was determined to stand with the Truth. From the day I was born, even through my illness, I had always chased after the Truth, after genuineness and authenticity, and now, right when the Truth needed the greatest support, I was not about to turn my back on it.

The ruling government had done a superb job in carrying exaggeration to a whole new level, over the top even, and had virtually engraved in the hearts and minds of the people that if this "coup" had been a successful one, then, the religion, all values and the whole country would have been destroyed. A major part of the society who were, apparently, only too eager to believe in a scenario like this were right there to support them. The volunteers of the Hizmet movement were now labeled as traitors and occupying forces. No one in their rightful mind stood up and asked why a fellow citizen would occupy its motherland, why would these people target their own religion, their own values? Even the oppositional political parties and other parts of society who were otherwise critical of the current government were silent. No one stood up to question what was really happening. Some were scared for themselves, others were just pleased, waiting to benefit from the wreckage. It was plain to see now that Turkey's real problem was fascism.

July 15 marked the beginning of a genocide. Every

day, thousands of innocent people, from artisans and shopkeepers to teachers and workers, to soldiers and policemen, people who had no connection with the attempted coup whatsoever, were being apprehended in their homes and forcibly taken away, some of whom were even killed shortly after they were taken into custody. Hizmet members were being excommunicated from the whole of society. Bigoted religious authorities refused to conduct any kind of religious ceremony for the individuals who had lost their lives. Some villagers refused to provide a burial ground for their fellow countrymen. There were so many people being taken under custody that stadiums and gymnasiums had been turned into mass detention halls. A state of emergency was declared all over the country. The ruling government had concocted a monster on the night of July 15 and was now shelving the constitutional laws in order to "combat" that monster. Those who were choosing to turn a blind eye to this grave injustice which for now only targeted one specific group were forgetting one very important detail. The rule of law was being trampled on in order to persecute the people of Hizmet today, but there was no guarantee that they wouldn't be needing it for themselves tomorrow...

"Pour some tea Keçeli and let's start anew..."

Using the chaos of July 15 as an excuse, the ruling government had snatched the awaited club in its hands, smashing it down on any critic or opposition it saw fit. A state of emergency was declared. The school I worked at, like all other institutions founded by the Hizmet movement, was locked up and shut down. The most convincing (!) argument the government put forth was this: members and volunteers of the Hizmet movement had - allegedly - established a secret terrorist organization known by the name FETO[5] and had attempted to take over the country and sell it out to others. So many allegations and accusations, none of which had any solid backing to it. Was there not a single person in their rightful mind that would please ask some basic questions like "How was Turkey going to be sold out? The people of Hizmet were secret spies of which countries??? What kind of sanctions would be put in place against those countries?" My mind was at a loss in comprehending this sociological case that was unfolding right in front of our eyes.

Chills were running down my spine. I prayed and

---

5 FETO is the name used by the current Erdogan government to describe the Hizmet movement. The Hizmet movement is based on moral values and advocacy of universal access to education, civil society, tolerance, and peace. For more information about the Hizmet movement, please visit www.afsv.org

prayed that the clouds of darkness suffocating us would clear away, yet no light could be seen at the end of the tunnel. Every day when I would hear of another friend being taken away and arrested, I was drowning deeper into sorrow. "But we haven't done anything wrong," I would say to myself, over and over. But most of the people around me did not think like me at all. "If they truly were innocent the government wouldn't be after them," they said. Some people had been so swept up into a war mentality that they had set up miniature arsenals in their homes, posting images of themselves armed with weapons, spewing out threats here and there. Worst of it all, hearing of rape incidents in the jails against our own brothers and sisters was so horrific I could not breathe.

The TV channels and news programs were so obsessed with news about FETO that it seemed as though no other newsworthy incident was happening throughout the whole country. Government leaders and authority figures were so enraptured in their quest for revenge that all they did, day and night, was spill out words of hatred and anger. "We are the law and what we say goes," was virtually what they were saying. The most tragic part of it all was that the people, the society, stood by and watched in excitement, as if watching an action movie on the big screen. The society had apparently lost their spirit of kindness and altruism altogether, a society that had begun to degrade, that had failed to understand the volunteers of goodness they had been living together with all this time. They had become so self-centered and interest-based that they did not believe anyone could do good just for the sake of doing good.

Those who knew me said, "Look Halime, we know you, you're a good person but it looks like those Hizmet people fooled you all this time." But that was not true! I knew my friends, and they were all good, clean, pure people. After the initial shock of it all, after realizing that there was some kind of conspiracy secretly brewing behind the whole ordeal, from that moment on, I decided to continue right where I had left off, on the path that I believed with all my heart to be the truth. After all, hadn't I found enlightenment through the books and works of an intellectual who had been made to spend thirty years of his life either in prison or in exile? Bediuzzaman Said Nursi[6], at a moment when it felt like they had lost

---

6 Bediuzzaman Said Nursi (1876-1960) lived through the decline of the Ottoman Empire, World War I and the emergence of the Turkish Republic. He is one of the most influential Islamic scholars in modern Turkish history. Nursi endured religious oppression and suffered through prolonged periods of exile and imprisonment. His followers reject political ambition, focusing instead on a revival of personal faith through study, self-reform, and service of others.

44

everything, had turned to his students and said, "Pour some tea *Keceli*, and let's start anew!" Now it was our turn to pour some tea and start anew. We were people of kindness and service, and we were certainly not about to give up on kindness and service, ever. Lanterns in hand, we would walk the streets through and through, pushing away the darkness and joyously awaiting the light of truth to rise up. There was much that needed to be done.

During that time, I had not lost touch with my old students, and I was following up on how they were and what they were doing. There was no way I could turn my back on the people I knew who were fluttering about like delicate butterflies amidst this fire that was raging on and surrounding us. At the time, I had not formed my own family yet; I had no spouse, no children. Thus, taking certain risks was much simpler for me...

In the beginning, I knocked on doors which, unfortunately, remained locked in my face. Everyone was leery of each other. The slander and the baseless accusations spreading throughout the country had stripped people of their trust in one another. So much so that you could think you were trying to help a friend, while that "friend" could secretly be reporting you to the police at the same time. But I didn't care. No matter how dire the circumstances, we would still do everything in our power to get in touch with old friends and bandage up the wounds of whoever was in need. Out-of-the-way corners in different shopping centers had become our go-to meeting spots. I was putting my life on the line, so to speak, walking around in a minefield. It was only yesterday we were living in a normal country, and now our home had turned into Nazi Germany. We were missing the gas chambers, but torture and death was raining on us nonetheless. If you ask me, were it not for social media and the internet, the gas chambers would certainly be there as well... Anyhow, one thing was for sure: the only thing these tyrants shied away from was having their savagery be discovered by the rest of the world.

Months passed... though the government assured the nation that the war of liberation they had started would make things better for everyone, things were not actually getting any better. Stability of any kind, be it material or spiritual, was absent from our lives. We had forgotten how to smile, and there was a constant tension in the air. On that dire night of July 15, our joy and love of life had been exterminated right along with the victims of that night. How pathetic that they were floundering to right their wrongs with other wrongs. There was no telling if they would ever be satisfied enough; if you ask me, they would eventually end up tearing each other apart (after they were done with everyone else). In prayer halls and mosques, pro-government religious leaders were instigating the people, crying out that the Hizmet members were infidels and that the people had a right to kill them and take their assets for their own. We were living through a real-life horror movie; a brain-washing virus had swept everyone under its effect.

Though my dear mother warned me several times, I did not pay much attention to her pleas. There were too many people in need of help. How could I possibly turn my back on the innocent children who were shunned even by their closest relatives after both parents had been arrested and jailed? I worked hard to determine the families on the brink of starvation and delivered groceries and financial aid to them. I had high school students that I took care of, kids whose parents had been arrested and who were suffering emotionally as a result of it. I went out to visit them with small gifts, trying as best I could to reassure them that they were not alone. Needless to say, none of these acts were done freely or lightheartedly. Murderers and thieves were brushed off to the side while all of the nation's police forces, in fact, even the MIT[7], were on the hunt for innocent people like me. Weaving through a different route each time, communicating over

---

7 Abbreviation of *Milli Istihbarat Teskilati*, Turkish State Intelligence Agency.

the internet and meeting in random parks, we found ourselves mastering techniques and tactics that would put secret service agents to shame. It felt as though our country was under occupation by enemy forces, and we were the dutiful citizens they wanted to annihilate. And what exactly was our crime? Picking up donations from a Good Samaritan and delivering them to a family in need? Surviving and trying to help others survive? Trying to find a new home for a needy family who was kicked out of their apartment? There were so many tasks that needed to be done. Oh, so many… Wasn't I afraid? Of course I was! We are talking of an atmosphere where people were being killed while they were being taken into custody, and then it simply being made to look like it was an accident. Being jailed, tortured, and killed were some of the things possibly awaiting me if I were to get caught. Yes, I was afraid, but my conscience trumped my fear. If I were to retreat into the comfort of my home and look out only for myself, yes, I might be able to avoid the tyrants, but what about my own conscience? There were souls out there longing for a loving greeting, souls who had been abandoned by their own relatives, neighbors, and friends. I was going to be the one to extend that greeting of love to whomever I could reach.

It was now over a year since the staged coup attempt

and things were just getting worse and worse with each passing day. How deep was the cliff that the country had fallen over that we fell and fell and yet, somehow, we just couldn't find the bottom?

The youngest of my three older brothers was living in Egypt. My dear mother, wanting to save me from the suffocating atmosphere of our home country, wanted to take me with her to Egypt for the birth of my nephew. I thought about it. A short visit was certainly doable. On July 5, 2017, we traveled to Egypt to visit my brother and his family. Having some time away from the chaos inside Turkey, stepping out for a change of atmosphere, felt really good. It felt like I had found my way out of a building in fire and finally could breathe. No venomous glances and hostile whispers from neighbors, no tensing up at the sight of a police officer; yet still my heart and mind were back home. I was ill-at-ease, couldn't get comfortable and cozy while so many of my friends and colleagues were suffering under baseless accusations. I had to go back. They say that no matter which path a person walks on, they are walking their destiny. And no matter what kind of life we lead, the only thing that awaits us at the end is our grave.

To my surprise, my family's intentions were a bit different. While in Egypt, they started saying things like how fortunate it was that I was actually able to make it out of Turkey and leave all problems behind; especially during a time in which even people with no search or arrest warrants in their name could easily be stopped at the airport and have their passports confiscated. Whereas here in Egypt I would be able to live freely and without worry. My dear mother could go back, close up the house, bring our things, and we could leave all the insanity behind us. They told me I was sitting right in the lion's mouth while living in Turkey, and it was only a matter of time until they came after me too. They said I'd be able to find work here in Egypt, that Hizmet movement was active here too, that I could even go on to another country if I wished to. What they were telling me made sense to my mind but not to my heart. With a calm but firm smile, I announced my decision. We had greeted my nephew into the world, and we had gone some sightseeing around Egypt; this was more than enough for me. I was going to go back to Turkey and continue to help all those who were suffering. The tasks that fell behind in my absence, the students who were left without a caretaker while I was in Egypt; it was already making me uneasy and restless. And thus, in August of 2017, we headed back into the deep and dark forest called Turkey, ruled over by evil-hearted villains and tyrants.

"Do people reckon that they will be left (to themselves at ease) on their mere saying, "We believe," and will not be put to a test?"

Chapter Ankabut - The Holy Qur'an

Back in Turkey, it was clear to see that the pressure and persecution against the Hizmet people had risen to a new level. The ruling government, dizzy from its insatiable thirst for power, was now labeling all other critics and opposing powers as part of the so-called FETO organization and was arresting them as well. Like I mentioned before, the coup scenario had been well received in the eyes of the general public. Arrests and apprehension continued, the witch hunt intensified by the minute. Nonetheless, I was determined to pick up where I left off in delivering help to whoever needed it. How could I possibly not? The number of people suffering had risen exponentially. People were left without jobs, without homes, without money; some were suffering from health problems, and all of them were helplessly waiting for a helping hand. Every morning I would grab my backpack with my daily dose of medicines in it, head out to a shopping center or a park somewhere and would spend time with my students. I would visit some of them in their homes, tutoring them, and helping with schoolwork. In fact, I would find out much later that after visiting one of my students in their home I had caught the attention of an undercover police officer who had already been following my student for some time, and they had started following me as well. It was December of 2017. I could feel someone's constant gaze on me as I would walk the streets. Dark shadows lurked in the dark corners, following every move I made. On one occasion when I was at the Mersin Mugdat Mosque, a man disguised as a janitor watched me from afar for an extended period of time, even took photos, and then left. I was now absolutely sure that they were keeping a close watch on me. And it looked like they felt no need to be discreet about it. I don't know whether it was the assurance that we were doing nothing illegal, but I didn't worry too much about it. "They're mistaken about what we're really about; once they see this for themselves and realize their mistake they'll give up harassing us," I thought. This nonsense had to end somewhere for sure! But it did not. If their oppression was a fire, their animosity was the wind raging it up. The wind kept on picking up speed, and the whole country had fallen crumbling into the heart of the flames. For them, the staged coup had been nothing but a showpiece excuse; the greater crime was to feel any kind of sympathy towards the Hizmet movement, and the designated punishment was total annihilation.

The people around us had conveniently silenced their ears to the atrocities surrounding them, going about their ordinary lives, caring for nothing more than their soccer matches and TV soap operas... they were acting like those I had once seen in a movie: bound by the spell of the evil witch, the people saw the bog as a delicious feast, feeding on the squirmy worms and critters as if they were eating the most delicious foods, and the few among them who had not been swept under the spell were trying to escape in horror. Believe me, with the exception of a small portion of the population who were uncomfortable with all that was happening, this was pretty much the situation our nation was suffering from. The public had been hypnotized to such a degree that they were unable to see that the real coup had been carried out against justice and the rule of law within the country. Everyone seemed to be content with their lives. Whereas, in fact, the ruling powers of the country were nothing more than a gang, lacking the concept of a functioning judiciary, wreaking havoc across the country.

January 2018 - If my mother would've known what would happen to me when she went to Canada to visit my other older brother, she certainly wouldn't have gone and left me behind. My sister-in-law had fallen seriously ill, and my brother had asked that my mother come and help out for a bit. She wanted me to tag along as well. To be honest, this time around I was actually leaning more positively towards getting out of the country. "All right," I said, "I'll come with you." I knew they were after me, and if I were to get arrested, there was no way I could help anyone anymore. Given the circumstances, it made more sense for me at that point to continue my efforts from afar. However, as luck would have it, I was denied a visa. After giving a lot of advice my mother left for Canada, and I stayed in Turkey. Apparently, the things I was meant to live through in Turkey were not over yet.

Other than an older brother living in the same neighborhood, I had no other close kin in the country. I continued with my everyday rush to aid the victims I knew. One night, about a month after my mother had left, towards the early dawn lights, I heard a heavy banging on the door. I jumped out of my bed in a flash and put on my clothes and *hijab*[8] as quickly as I could. Well, it was the inevitable finale knocking at my door. Interestingly, with my mother gone, I hadn't been staying at home much those days. I would stop by from time to time, picking up a few items I needed and going on to stay with friends. I could

---

8 Arabic word, refers to head coverings worn by Muslim women. While Islamic head coverings can come in many forms, *hijab* often specifically refers to a cloth wrapped around the head and neck, covering the hair but leaving the face visible.

very well not have been at home that night either, but I was. Was I scared as the banging on the door continued nonstop? Yes, but not to an extreme. I knew there was no standing in the way of what was bound to happen one day. I believed in the will of Allah with all my being. I was completely at ease, with a clear conscience. The way I could keep calm in the face of such encounters was something even my friends would find odd on occasion.

It was February 20, 2018 – The Anti-Terror Special Forces team of Mersin were standing at my door, armed with heavy artillery. I grabbed the phone and called my brother who lived close by. I told him the police were at my door; I wanted to let him know just in case. They kept banging on the door nonstop until I was finally dressed and able to open the door. If a couple more minutes had passed, I'm sure they would have forced their way in. As soon as the door was open, they pushed me to the side, and a whole team of policemen entered in; whereas in all honesty, just one of them would have been perfectly sufficient to escort me to the station. Their behavior towards me was so hostile, as though I was a terrible creature from outer space to destroy their country. I, too, was a citizen of this country, wasn't I? For hours they searched every nook and cranny in the house. They practically turned the house upside down. As if that were not enough, they stomped on my personal possessions which they had carelessly thrown all over the floor. They yelled at me, cursed at me. From the pots and pans in the kitchen, to the boxes of dried goods in the pantry, to even the potting soil of the flowers in my home, they searched and searched. Not because they thought they were going to actually find something, mind you; this was all just a part of their show of power, a kind of harassment, an attempt to intimidate and break me down. My guess was that the rewards and gratifications they received increased in proportion to the degree of rudeness and aggression they displayed on the job. "Why don't you go and search for your consciences and minds that you've all obviously lost?" my inner voice cried out at them. For hours I watched them throw our things on the floor and kick about at our clothes and undergarments. Their heavy weapons, the way they constantly spoke into their radios as if they were carrying out a high-risk operation, it was all so pathetic I wanted to laugh out loud. From the looks of it, they probably must have thought I was going to grow extra arms and teeth out of my body and attack them. It truly was ridiculous. I doubt that even murderers who have actually killed people in cold blood would be subject to such harassment. In fact, this wasn't just me doubting; I saw it on the news and media every day. As for me, I took refuge in my only sanctuary, my dear Lord, and patiently waited for them to be done and leave me and my home in peace.

Despite not having found a single item that could be passed off as an element of a crime, they continued with their slander and cursing and said they would be taking me into custody. This was not something they had told me up front, and I was not prepared for it. I asked for permission to call my brother to let him know that I was being taken in and to ask him to bring me a new supply of medicines that I have been using, but they refused. They said I could call him up later. I asked for a couple minutes to gather up the things that I would need to have with me. They said no. They were in such a hurry to take me away that I was only able to throw a couple things into my purse which I happened to come across. I quickly threw in a couple of clothing items, my daily medicine and my health report into my bag. It was February 20, 2018, and I was handcuffed and taken out of my home under police custody.

This was how my adventure in captivity began. The search that had begun at morning prayer time (dawn) had continued until 9 am. I was surrounded by police, my hands were cuffed, and I was being escorted out of my home. I didn't know then that this was not going to be a round trip. As I breathed in the cool morning air, I took a long look around. The world was waking up to a beautiful winter morning. As we walked over to the police car, there were a couple of neighbors out on the street watching us with an uneasy glance. The police pushed my head down as I got in the car. My days of freedom were thereby coming to an end. Inside the car, I turned around to take one last look at our home. How lonely and mournful it looked. A few tears streaked down my cheeks as memories floated through my mind. Having to leave behind the home that had served us for so many years, in such a disheveled state was just too heavy on my heart at that moment...

To tell the truth, I had mentally prepared myself for anything that could happen. Whatever was written in my destiny was the will of my Lord, and I was not about to object to any of it. Still, being treated in a way that I did not deserve burned me on the inside; like I had drunk poison. The hands which I raised to the heavens every day to pray for the peace and prosperity of this nation were now being cuffed together, and I was being taken into the unknown. These policemen whom I had never before seen in my life...why were they so angry at me? I prayed and prayed to my Lord to protect me from the evil of these men who thought they were doing service to their country by pushing around a frail and weak woman and kicking and stomping on her belongings. We passed through the streets I had once carelessly walked through, only this time I was being taken through like a prisoner of war. I was being treated like dangerous vermin. The rose gardens we grew up in had turned into a swamp land. If I did not have my faith, I would not have had the strength to bear all this. I firmly believed that through God's will we had lived such joyful, such wonderful times in the past years, doing service to others and enjoying beauty and blessings as part of this worldly life. And now, again through God's will, we were passing through days of darkness and dread. This was clearly a test we had to get through as part of this life. I prayed to my Lord that He would give me the strength to endure it all and push through it. This too would pass.

For the sake of formality, we had to go through a doctor's exam at the health clinic. Upon entering the doctor's office I wanted to bring to his attention that I suffered from a chronic illness; however the doctor was far from interested and merely motioned for me to exit as he signed the paperwork sitting on his desk. The other patients waiting in the hallways moved to the side as we passed through. Some of them shouted out insults at me as we passed.

Our next stop was a filthy detention cell, its walls and floor covered in dirt and grime. Before handing over my purse to the police officers, I searched it inside and out, over and over again, only to discover that I had left behind my weekly medicine. I had to talk to my brother and have him bring me my medicine as soon as possible. Once we were at the detention center, they took hold of everything I had brought with me, including my health report. During the entire time I was kept in the detention center, I was denied any communication with my brother. I learned much later that all the while he had been searching for me, going from one police station to another. They had me sign a document which stated that my brother had been informed of my whereabouts; whereas, in fact, he had not been notified of anything. My brother had no idea where I was or what had become of me.

It was only the first day, and I was already tired out. We were all hungry, thirsty and worried. Most of the others who were in custody were there because of the same reason I was. This was our first encounter in our lives with a law officer or a police station; a group of glowing, naive women who were so unfit to be locked behind iron bars. There were quite a number of us in there. I already knew some of them. Apparently, that morning they had simultaneously "busted" many different addresses. A hundred or more "terrorists" (!) had been apprehended, and they had once more saved the country from our evilness! But if you asked us, our only agenda was how we would ever be able to make our ablutions and perform our daily prayers here. A couple of women who were in there because of petty crimes were standing at a distance and whispering among one another. I would guess that this was not a scene they were used to seeing.

In the detention cell, in that icy cold room where there was no proper space to sit down, we were made to wait an ambiguous wait. Each one of us recited prayers we knew with fluttering hearts. Many of the women were worried sick about their children who were left behind. We tried to console one another, repeating over and over that there must be a grave mistake and that our innocence would be clarified very soon. We were clean, both in the eyes of the law and in the depths of our consciences. However, what had not occurred to us at all was the extent of the audacity of the ruling government, which pretty much had already tried and sentenced us. We were kept there in the detention center for thirteen days straight. Not a single soul stopped to listen to my plight, and I was unable to get hold of the weekly medicine I desperately needed to take. What's more, my health report explaining my illness was lost there too, vanished into thin air somehow…

"He who thinks that he knows all the answers has not been asked all the questions."

Confucius

Time stood still in the detention cell. As we closed in on a week in that dark, damp and dirty hole, it started to feel like I had been living there my whole life. I'm guessing one of the reasons for that is that the only real truth for a person is the present moment in which they are in at the time. Another reason is that a grueling moment can expand and overwhelm to such an extent that even memories start losing clarity and actuality. I came to understand this very well in that filthy place where even drinking a glass of clean water was an impossibility; let alone lying down and getting a good night's sleep.

At the end of the thirteen days when we were finally taken to the courthouse to appear before a judge, I was more than ready for whatever verdict would be given, so long as I didn't have to go back to that filthy hole. The prosecutor offered me a chance to benefit from what they called the "effective remorse law" saying that if I gave them names from within the Hizmet (he used the word FETO, of course) I would be let go with no penalty. "It's up to you," he said, "you can make the choice to sleep in your warm bed tonight." If snatching an innocent person away from their home and family was what it took for me to get back to my own, I did not want it. "I have no connections whatsoever with a terrorist organization," I said and refused their offer. Neither I nor any person I knew had committed any crime. What was I to show remorse for?! Which fellow colleague, friend or poor man/woman was I supposed to give the name of??

Shocking as it was, I personally was not alarmed over where things had led. My sorrow and worry was for my friends who had no one to care for their children when they were gone. The so-called coup of July 15 was obviously neither head nor tail, just a wreaking of havoc meant to destroy the lives of myself and others like me. The crime they were charging me with was the fact that I had provided financial and emotional support to the true victims of all this chaos, especially the children and youth whose families had been taken into custody. Not only did the government officials turn their backs on these children, but they also wanted to make sure to cut off any support from us as well. Of course, they knew very well how to play with the words and make it sound like an actual crime; "providing financial support to a terrorist organization", they called it. But however you looked at it, this accusation was nothing but a crazed absurdity. Under normal circumstances, the acts for which I was now being accused would be considered a real virtue. Needless to say, I objected. I told them that I had committed no crime, that I was a patient with a chronic illness and that prison conditions posed a great risk for my well-being. The judge being a woman had raised my expectations that she would approach my case with more empathy, but she remained indifferent and cold, looking down on me from her castle of ice. Upon my persistence, she looked at me like I was a piece of garbage standing in her path and asked, "Do you have the related health documents?" Here I was, unable to prove that I was sick because the health report I had submitted to the Anti-Terror Police officers had somehow gotten lost (!) at the station. If I had that report to submit during the trial, there may have been a way for me to be released according to the law. Come to think of it, if they had wanted to, both the police and the prosecutor could have easily gotten hold of my report by simply requesting a copy from the health institution where I had been given the report initially.

And the awaited decision! As the judge read the decision to arrest to my face, I felt like I was falling, falling into a deep, deep well. She, on the other hand, was as devoid of any kind of emotion as she could be. Like stone, like ice... Here I stood, in the same small room with this person stripping me of my freedom, and it felt like we stood galaxies apart. She did not care the least bit about who I really was, what I had been through, what my story was. Every single word that took flight off the paper she held in her hand landed like a gavel pounding into my brain. I was being arrested by the Mersin 4th Peace Court on March 3, 2018, on the charges of membership to the FETO armed terrorist organization and providing financial support to the organization. When finished, the judge grumbled that I needed to exit the courtroom right away because many others were waiting in line. It was like a heavy curtain had fallen over the eyes of these pro-dictator servants who so easily and unbelievably condemned us as traitors and terrorists.

As I passed my destiny-sisters waiting out in the corridor, I could not help but remark: "Whoever wants to see a terrorist with no criminal record and no weapon, let them have a long look at us, my dear friends."

"They arrested you?!" my friend asked in shock. The only thing I could do was force a bitter smile... At that moment, I looked into my heart to reflect. What was it that I truly felt at this point? First of all, I felt shame for my country. A nation that had been the founding ground of such well rooted civilizations should not have ended up in such a state. It had given birth to a monster out to devour its own children. Everything had been turned upside down. The very enforcers of the rule of law were blazing the trail in lawlessness and the absence of law. Some attempted to explain this utterly bizarre situation as the whole country being put under a spell of some kind or other. They said it could be witchcraft, something in the city water supply or the bread or something… We were completely lost trying to figure out a rational explanation as to why the neighbors, relatives, and friends who we walked arm in arm with only days ago, were now treating us like dangerous creatures sent down from outer space.

It felt like I was being pushed wildly downstream, caught up in an angry river that rushed on with no mercy. The only member of my family living in Turkey was my brother, even he did not have a clue as to where I was or what was happening to me. Like I mentioned before, we hadn't had a chance to see each other during the whole time I was held in custody. No one had bothered to notify my brother. It was the lawyer of a friend in custody who had notified my brother of my arrest, long after it all happened.

And as the iron doors of the Tarsus prison opened for me to enter, it turned out that it was the beginning of the final stage of my short worldly life here on Earth. Gendarmerie, guards, clinks of iron bars, slander and insults, these had become the decor of this new stage of my life.

The adventure started with a three-day stay in the temporary ward section, under horrible conditions that could not be any further from proper hygiene. A freezing cold cell so filthy, so disgusting, you wouldn't want to touch even a corner of it with the tip of your fingers. I asked for a glass of drinking water and was immediately snapped at by the guard, saying I could drink water from the faucet in the toilet. But the problem was, I needed clean drinking water regularly in order to take my medicine. Others asking for drinking water had also been treated with such bitterness. Those who drank from the faucet, however, had suffered from stomachaches and abdominal pain which further developed into diarrhea. Finally, at the end of the three days, we were taken to the ward where we would actually be staying. Because we had had to endure such horrible conditions for sixteen days straight, actually being charged and arrested and knowing what would become of us almost felt like we were being set free and, as tragicomic as it may seem, we almost rejoiced. At least, I was finally going to have my own bed, or so I hoped, and I would have a chance to take my ablution and perform my prayers in some level of comfort. And tea... I would finally get to enjoy some tea...maybe...

As I was taken away by guards, I clutched tightly to my bag which held the few belongings I had with me. We passed through one iron gate after another, leaving behind corridor after corridor. Like a confused child, I walked on surrounded by filthy walls and feeling as uneasy as ever. The guards, on the other hand, carelessly hummed their favorite folk songs as they buried me under layers and layers of stone walls. Their hearts were like stones, cold stares in their eyes…

They opened the door of the ward, motioned for me to get inside, and locked the door behind me. Is this where I would be staying? As I stood there not knowing what to do and looking around blankly, a couple of women walked towards me. It was written all over their faces, we all shared the same story, the same destiny. One of them was the ward leader. She opened her arms and greeted me with such a warm embrace that it helped to shake off some of my anxiety. It turns out that actually they didn't want any newcomers into the ward anymore. The ward was filled with double the capacity as it was, and it was nearly impossible to breathe in this tiny, closed-up room. Well, getting to sleep in a bed that belonged to me was once again not going to be so easy.

The ward I found myself in was a two-story space, with a single bathroom and toilet, and the capacity to hold ten people. With my addition, the population of the ward was now over twenty people. Each one of my fellow inmates, with shining faces and gentle as ever, had all been subject to the same injustice as I had been. Very quickly, I became acquainted with them and each one of our stories pretty much lined up with one another. Each one of these women who were being accused of being traitors and terrorists were all well-educated and true patriots. Our terrorism was the terrorism of a person who even took shame in throwing a single piece of garbage on the street, let alone commit any crime of any kind. Among my fellow inmates, there were highly qualified and highly educated women who had studied abroad and trained themselves well. As I looked at each one, I couldn't help but think what a grave loss it was for the country that these women were locked behind bars. The sorrow was overwhelming. There was a lieutenant governor of a city who, after being elected the first district governor in Turkey, had led the way for many significant projects to be completed in Eastern Anatolia. There was a police chief who was a criminal expert and probably the best in the field. There was a criminal court judge who had won the admiration of those around her for her dedicated work ethic. I must say, through all the things I personally witnessed in that ward, these women were not people to harm their country. On the contrary, they would raise it to greater heights.

The first days of prison life were truly very difficult. One may have to endure many different hardships and tests throughout a lifetime, but I would argue that prison life was on a completely different scale. In the beginning, it feels like someone has wound a rope over and over around your throat, suffocating you, leaving you breathless until your lungs burn from lack of air. You're scared stiff; terrified at the thought of having to live from that point on in a place where you're not even sure how to live. Not to mention the ill-treatment by the guards, who treated us like prisoners of war. The Tarsus prison was, after all, famous for the torture and harsh treatment of its inmates.

Thankfully, within about a week, I started adapting more to the environment. Still, this was not where I belonged. Because of my illness my immune system was very fragile; I needed to be living in a sterile environment. But here, I was deprived of clean air, hearty nourishment, and high spirits. There were so many of us, living in such tight quarters. If one person caught a cold or the flu, it would spread to us all. In other words, it wasn't only the absence of my medicine that was compromising my health. Upon learning about my health condition and how I was unable to reach my health report and the medicine I needed, my dear fellow inmates, whose own sorrows could be read from their eyes, forgot about their own problems, set aside their own wounds, and they tried to comfort me and cheer me up. Here we were, twenty-two individuals, in a ten-person ward. And two kids. The prison ward was so congested that the system was two-to-a-bed, and the beds were so small they had to be kid-size.

Prison conditions are naturally, in one way or another, challenging and difficult for anyone who finds themselves locked behind bars. However, for those of us labeled as "FETO members," it was so much more... It was like we were in another prison within the prison. Opportunities given to the other inmates, even to the murderers and thieves, were all denied to us "FETO members." Using the gym, participating in the courses/classes that were offered, watching a movie with others every now and then in a designated room in the prison…these were all forbidden. Some of our friends who had inquired about it had been answered straight out: "Nothing for you!" We were "FETO members," the suspects in the Parallel State investigations… Oh the crimes that had been conjured up in our honor! For the love of God, could someone please explain to me what kind of accusation was this…a Parallel State Structure?! People working legally and only doing their jobs in the state-owned institutions…how could and why would these people form a parallel state? If the issue was the world-view and political opinions of these individuals, then shouldn't every single individual who worked at a state-owned institution and who happened to hold a different political opinion and ideology be accused of attempting to establish a "Parallel State Structure"? Didn't every person, in one way or another, hold a unique world-view and have some kind of ideal of their own? Come to think of it, it was the ruling government in Turkey who was perpetrating the very thing that they were accusing us of...a gang of thieves with no other ideal than money, power and position... They were the epitome of what a Parallel State Structure was!

If the soul is truly enlightened, then no dungeon can bury it into darkness...

Life was teaching me something new every single day. One of the many things it taught me during my days in prison was this: Where a person is of some importance; however, what's more important is *how* a person is. The ability to turn every situation into an achievement, a personal gain, is in the hands of the individual, no matter what situation they find themselves in. For instance, they may have locked us behind bars, surrounded by concrete walls, but this did not mean that we were going to sit around and wait to rot away. This period of time spent away from the hullabaloo of everyday life and responsibilities was an opportunity for us to work on bettering ourselves. A journey to the inside, disciplining one's heart and soul... these were of crucial importance for a believer, and this forced reclusion may be the perfect environment we needed to achieve this.

Here is a rundown of what our daily program looked like: At 8 am, we would gather out in the courtyard for roll-call. Afterward, anyone who had a written petition or letter to be sent would pass it on to the guard, and everyone would return to their wards. After roll-call, we would buy some food items from the canteen for breakfast, eat and then prepare for mid-morning prayers.

We would take turns praying because the praying area we were able to set up on the second-floor of the ward could only accommodate one person at a time. While we took turns praying in the small prayer area, the others read from the Holy Qur'an and other books. After the prayer around noon, we would go down to the first floor to see what kind of food was brought for the day. If the food looked completely inedible, we would pass the day with some salad and tuna fish we bought from the canteen. After lunch, it would be the awaited tea time. Complete with a hot cup of tea, some would cozy back up in their beds continuing to read from where they had left off, others would enjoy their tea with a good chat. We would perform the afternoon prayer and then continue reading. Following the evening prayer, we would go back out for the evening roll-call. The guards with their harsh orders and instructions would rush to finish up and get it over with. We would stand single file in the courtyard and start counting: one, two, three...twenty-one, twenty-two. Say, I was eighteen one day, for instance... For them, I was only "eighteen." That "eighteen" did not involve my increasing nausea, my exhaustion, my crushed hopes and dreams...That "eighteen" was just a number, it was not *me*. Our innocence, our broken hearts, the most powerful and moving words that flowed from our tongues... none of it reached them. As a matter of fact, there were some verses in the Qur'an that made specific reference to such situations. If Allah did not will it, ears could not hear, minds could not comprehend, and people would look but not see. As I watched the careless and fearless attitude in which the guards carried out their cruelty and abuse I started fearing for myself; I prayed to Allah to never leave me to be as blind and deaf as these people had become.

When the human being is the subject matter at hand, an exact calculation like "two and two is four" almost never holds. You can have a group of people with the same exact opportunities, means, or hardships, and you will still find that some will be happy while others will not. When our Lord wills, most certainly He can place Heaven inside Hell. Here we were, through His Mercy and Grace, locked in a dungeon of darkness, yet we were still able to fill with Light. We were overwhelmed with sorrow and heartbreak, yet still our hearts were filled with contentment. For one thing, our consciences were at ease. We were not the ones doing the hurting, we were the ones being hurt. This fleeting worldly life was going to end one way or another. And our biggest hope was that this undeserved prison life would serve as atonement for our sins and would purify us.

We had a system set up to take turns taking care of

cleaning and kitchen duty. In the evenings, we would spread one of the blankets out on the floor, cover it with plastic trash bags, lay out a smorgasbord of treasured finds from the canteen, accompanied by a pot of tea, and we would sit round and chat away. Some evenings we would read a passage from the Risale-i Nur[9] collection and engage in an insightful lesson on belief. Some evenings we would read from other books we had available. Everyone would find something to keep busy with until about eleven or so. Depending on my mood and energy, some nights I would get out my tatting shuttle to embroider with or orlon thread to make bracelets. As I worked with my hands, I would remember the days when my dear mother had taught me and how much fun we had, and I would just smile as I remembered. I would close my eyes and try to imagine that I was sitting in our living room. I would feel the gentle breeze flowing in through the open window and listen to the joyous chatter of the children playing right outside. They say the soul is not limited to time and

---

9 Collection of the books written by Said Nursi. Rather than being a Quranic commentary which expounds all its verses giving the immediate reasons for their revelation and the apparent meanings of the words and sentences, the Risale-i Nur is a commentary which expounds the meaning of the Quranic truths. The verses mostly expounded in the collection of the Risale-i Nur are those concerned with the truths of belief, such as the divine names and attributes and the divine activity in the universe, the divine existence and unity, resurrection, Prophethood, divine determining or destiny, and man's duties of worship.

space, that it is free to roam wherever it wishes. And so, I would take a little outing with it, from time to time.

From eleven to about midnight we would have an hour of prayer time. We would read passages from the Holy Qur'an and the Jawshan[10]. The ward would fill with the sound of sobbing, my friends and I crying our hearts out in front of our Lord. Bent over in front of our Lord, feeling weak and incompetent like small children, our lips would curl, our necks would fall, and we sobbed, not for our own selves; we sobbed for our fellow brothers and sisters. We sobbed for our sister who had to send her newborn baby home to her husband because the prison conditions threatened her baby's well-being, and how she had to pump her baby's milk out into the faucet instead of her baby's mouth where it belonged, and how she sent it flowing down the drain mixed with the tears that she could not hold back any longer. We sobbed for our sisters who, no matter how hard they tried, could not come to terms with the injustice that had been done to them and how they considered taking their own life just to end it all. Like the great poet Nazım Hikmet[11] said in his poem,

---

10 *Jawshan* is a long Islamic prayer that contains the names and attributes of God.

11 Nazım Hikmet (15 January 1902 – 3 June 1963) is a Turkish poet, playwright, novelist, screenwriter, and director. He was repeatedly arrested for his political beliefs and spent much of his adult life in prison or in exile. His poetry has been translated into more than fifty languages.

"How do I not fill with sorrow when I think of the plight of my people; they fight for dear life trampled under the feet of a few scoundrels." We sobbed for our country and our people. We sobbed for the good works that were no longer, we sobbed for the youth that was left with no one to protect them and look after…

As for me… The fact that I was not able to take some of my meds combined with the harsh living conditions had taken a toll on my body. I had lost a lot of weight. A task as simple as walking could leave me tired and weak. My friends were worried about me. I can easily say that even I wasn't as worried as they were. I had never been one to take the world too seriously anyway. Good days couldn't cheer me up very much; bad days couldn't depress me. Everything was becoming history so fast, anyhow.

After the clock struck twelve, those who wished to sleep would go up to the second-floor of the ward where it was lights-out. Nonetheless, the Holy Qur'an would be recited non-stop through the night on the bottom floor. The bottom floor was designated for our friends who wished to pray their nightly prayers and read until the morning light. I couldn't help but think sometimes, "Could it be that our dear Lord had gathered us all here because we somehow had not set aside the proper time for our worship on account of the hullabaloo of worldly life?" Perhaps He was telling us, "What I asked of you was for you to be dutiful servants above and before everything else!" Like everyone else around me, I too was trying to figure out what the meaning was of us being locked behind bars, our wrists bound by cold hand-cuffs…

We completed the reading of the Holy Qur'an from cover to cover on a weekly basis and the Jawshan on a daily basis. Like with all the other tasks around the ward, my friends would take special care not to tire me out too much. "Halime, you can read a shorter passage," they would say. They treated me with great care, like I was a porcelain doll. On days when I didn't have the energy to even lift a finger, I would just sit and watch these women with admiration. I felt content to be among them.

During our prison days, we would experience certain events, from time to time, that could not be explained in rational terms. Let me tell you about one of these experiences. So, it was already nothing short of a miracle that twenty-plus individuals were able to shower and do their laundry all within the 5-6 hours a day when hot water was available, but we managed somehow. We would hang our laundry to dry on the couple of lines out in the courtyard and would usually have to pick them up before they were fully dry so others could use them, too. Well, one day, before my friends had a chance to gather up their clothes from the clothesline, the guards had ushered everyone inside and locked the doors to the courtyard. Naturally, this was a great disappointment for my friends who had their clothes out there because if it happened to rain at night, they would have to go through the whole process of rewashing and re-drying their laundry. As you can probably guess, it rained cats and dogs that night. The next morning when we went out at 8 am for the morning roll-call, I too witnessed the scene that had everyone astonished. The ground was wet, but the clothes and the boxes of food items were dry. The boxes which held essential food items like onions and garlic, etc. were dry, whereas other trivial and miscellaneous items that stood to the side were waterlogged. This sure seemed like a divine gift to me, but of course, our Lord knows best.

Sometimes they'll take away everything and leave you empty-handed, so those hands can open up in ardent prayer...

Days passed, yet there was no positive development regarding my weekly medicine and my health report. I could not prove for certain that my report had been lost intentionally; however, there was no doubt that we were surrounded by excessive neglect and malice. We were trapped in the hands of those who believed that everything about us should be wiped out. They treated us as if even the air we breathed was a waste, as if it was through their grace they were allowing us to go on living. Like a handful of survivors on a sunken boat, we were flailing around to keep our heads above water, to keep from drowning altogether. Judging by the words trickling from the mouths of the prison officers, the best-case scenario was that we were all doomed to rot here, and that we deserved every second of it. No matter what they said, I believed with all my heart that just as my Lord saved Prophet Jonah from the belly of the whale, if it were His will, He would save us too, and He would restore our human dignity and our honor. Come to think of it, that they have turned our short worldly life into misery was not that great a deal. We believed in the eternal Afterlife, and there was not a trace of a doubt that the trial to be held there would be of absolute justice.

Never had I hurt or been unjust or unfair with anyone, yet I was being subject to such horrible treatment, but I knew that everyone responsible would be called on to account one day. During the beginning of our confinement, there had been a rotavirus case that had spread throughout the whole ward. We all suffered from vomiting, diarrhea, stomachaches, and abdominal pain... Buckled up and cringing in a corner of the ward, we begged the guards to let us go up to the infirmary. They split us into two groups and took us in for a quick IV therapy. That was it, a bag of IV fluids and then we were left to tackle the virus on our own. It would take at least a week for the prescribed medicine to arrive anyhow. There was a 10-month-old baby living with us in the ward. The virus first settled in the baby's body and from there had spread to the rest of us. Another baby, a 3-month-old, had been hit so badly by the virus that her life had been endangered. When the mother saw that her baby might not make it through these prison conditions, she had no other choice but to send her baby back to her hometown of Maras when her father came to visit. The cries of a nursing mother separating from her baby were so heart-wrenching that it took us days to recover. That poor woman's only crime was that she had deposited a small amount of money into a bank that had been operating legally under government inspection for years; she was sentenced to two years of prison confinement[12].

I had friends in the ward who had been making requests for four months, and they still hadn't been sent to the infirmary for a check-up. I, too, kept writing up requests to be seen by a doctor, but there was no answer. Some of the inmates had high-blood pressure, heart problems, or diabetes... One of our friends developed uterine cancer, and they finally released her. There were so many of us being mistreated and neglected...

Every second I spent in that stuffy, overcrowded ward reflected poorly on my health. Yes, it was true, my belief in fate was strong. But having faith also meant that I was obligated to preserve the health of the body my Lord had entrusted to me. Taking precautions and fulfilling whatever means necessary to do so was also a part of living out my faith. And so, for this precise reason,

---

12 Tens of thousands of individuals were trialed in "July 15 related" courts, most of them were found guilty and sentenced for imprisonment, for the acts which did not constitute a criminal offense under the law in force at the time it was committed, or even at the time of those trials. Some of those so-called "criminal offenses" were being subscribed to the best-selling newspaper in Turkey, Zaman, which was in circulation since 1986; having an account in Bank Asya, which was one of the biggest banks in Turkey since 1996; and choosing the schools affiliated with Hizmet Movement for your children to attend. Inviting your friends to your house or visiting them in their houses on a regular basis was also considered a crime.

right from the very first day I had been locked behind these rusty iron bars, I had been striving hard to access the necessary treatment and health care I needed.

My legs and knees were weak with exhaustion, yet I exerted myself to stand up straight as I handed over yet another written request to the guard at the door, in order to be seen for a check-up at the infirmary... The sullen-faced guard took the papers and carelessly walked on, saying I would just have to wait my turn. Thus, my first chance to visit the infirmary took about 10-12 days after being admitted to the ward. When you add the time spent in the initial detention room, it totaled up to nearly a month-long wait. Yet my illness was of a kind where even a minute was considered precious time.

Meanwhile, my brother brought another copy of my health report that had gotten lost the first time around, but that second copy also ended up being lost. "This is just plain inexcusable!" my friends exclaimed. I kept my calm, because, let's face it, we had already seen that practically anything could be possible. After July 15, nothing was impossible anymore. There were innocent people being tortured mercilessly, being killed in cold blood, being treated with such injustice you wouldn't wish it for your worst enemy. And it wasn't only those who had been arrested. There were thousands of Hizmet volunteers still outside, some who had been abandoned by their friends and family, others being denied work or any way of providing for themselves and their families. A part of us suffered on one side of the iron bars, while another part of us suffered on the other side. I thought and thought about why all this was happening. There was only one thing I could be certain of. If my Lord allowed those perpetrating such atrocities to keep on breathing, then He must certainly have a Divine Purpose, a Will that was in process, and what I needed to do was to prepare myself for that.

Days later, I finally received a response to my written requests. It was the 14th of March, 2018. I was finally going to see a doctor. Here's what ended up happening: the doctor in the prison infirmary pretty much scolded me, "You look fine, why are you here?" I spoke to the doctor about the nature of my illness and how I had been grappling with it for the past fifteen years. If they had been able to look me up in the healthcare database system, then surely my condition would be apparent. However, for whatever reason, the system had crashed down. One misfortune after another...as if all outside elements had united and were leading me to a specific destination.

"Well, if you're really that sick, what business do you have getting involved in these terrorist activities?" they asked, as if somehow justifying that I deserved no mercy. Nonetheless, even if it was just to be rid of me, even if it was done half-heartedly, the prison doctor did send a note to the gendarmerie for me to be taken to a hospital for a check-up, at the general internal medicine department. This certainly was something.

Two days later, at the Tarsus Public Hospital general internal disease department, I was seen by a doctor who conducted a pretty superficial, quick check-up. I asked to be sent to the rheumatology department, which was specifically where I needed to be seen by a specialist, but my request was denied. My personal request carried no credit for them. The doctor asked for some bloodwork, and I was taken to the lab to give blood sample. Maybe, just maybe, the pieces would fall into place. The results of the bloodwork would reveal the reason behind all the nausea, acute exhaustion, aches, and cramps. As someone grappling with such a serious illness, just maybe I would finally be released. Upon returning to the prison ward, all my friends hugged me and reassured me with hopeful words. They were all so happy for me…

Tasks like following up on doctor appointments, taking test results to the doctor to be evaluated, picking up prescriptions and other meds were all under the responsibility of the guards. A few days after my appointment with the doctor, the guard appointed to my case took my test results up to the doctor to be evaluated. When the guard called out my name at the door of the ward, I quickly walked over in hopeful anticipation. Unfortunately, there was not a sign of hope in the way she stood there in the doorway, face sullen as can be, a shaking of the head as though reprimanding me. According to what she said, the specialist doctor had seen the results of the lab tests and said that everything looked normal and healthy. "There's nothing wrong with you. You keep complaining that you're sick, you're only wasting our time," she grumbled, practically throwing the results at my face. I felt like I'd just been punched in the face. It was already obvious that the staged July 15 coup had been done to wipe off the Hizmet movement. And now we were being struck with grief and disaster every single day; we were the ones being trampled upon and beaten. The rulers of the country who cried out about having been victimized through the coup attempt were only growing stronger day by day, while we were the ones falling and being scattered, like autumn leaves in the harsh wind...

I was stupefied by the shock of what I was hearing. My hands shook as I tried to gather up the scattered papers and said "What are you talking about? What does this all mean...that I'm making up an illness for myself? I'm sick, I tell you, my health is deteriorating every day!" They never had liked us using the word "guard" to refer to them...we had to call them as "corrections officers!" They were nothing but gatekeepers of hell! And so, the guard turned around and left, just like that. Her mean attitude was one thing, but still, I couldn't stop myself from thinking... "What if? What if this sickness I felt was all in my head? Could it be that I was indeed healthy? Perhaps the lupus was really inactive?" Oh, how I would've loved to be proven wrong, to have this illness go away and never come back. But then, why was it that I was losing so much weight?

As soon as the guard had left, my friends gathered around and started showering me with questions. They were concerned about my well-being. "It turns out I'm healthy, turns out I went to the doctor for nothing..." I said with a bittersweet smile. They too were mesmerized. "But how can it be?" they said. As I walked over to the small closet to put away the papers, something did not feel right. I settled down quietly on the corner of my bed and started looking through the test results one by one. In the past, for so many years, I had been through the routine bloodwork procedures so many times that I knew what everything meant by heart. As I turned the pages and looked over the results, it became clearer and clearer that these were not the bloodwork needed for my illness. These were the results of a basic routine check-up like blood-cell count etc. I stood up and cried out, "This is not the bloodwork for my illness! They didn't even request the necessary bloodwork; they never even took a look at it!" This disappointment was so overwhelming that it felt like I was drowning in a bottomless well, and the more I tried to climb up and out of it, the deeper I found myself falling and falling... In all honesty, even without the tests and the bloodwork, anyone who cared enough to take a good look at me would see that I was not well, I was withering away and the light had gone out of my eyes.

"Even when a tyrant oppresses, the Divine Destiny executes Justice."

Bediuzzaman Said Nursi

My friends were more grieved than I was at the fact that my hospital visit had ended up a dead end. They couldn't hide their worries and kept reminding me that I needed to immediately write up another request to go back to the hospital. The legal experts among us reminded me about my legal rights and others expressed their rage and stood in solidarity with my plight. "If the rule of law had any meaning, which one of us would be here right now?" I only said with a half-smile. Touched by their motherly fretting over me, I tried to reassure them that I was fine. The fact that I was smiling while my body was deteriorating more and more every day was kind of bizarre for them. I would guess that some of them could not comprehend why and how in the world I could stay so calm. There were some who kept telling me that I should speak up louder, that I should cry out, "I'm dying in here!" and that I should be throwing myself on the floor or nothing would ever change. And they were right.

However, that kind of loud and aggressive behavior was not something I could bring myself to do. I did the only thing I could do. With my shaking fingers, I picked up paper and pen and decided to write another request to once again be seen by the doctor. Meanwhile, in another corner of the ward, a group of our friends were working hard in our makeshift "kitchen." One of our biggest handicaps here was the food which was pretty tasteless and served in small portions, and so we tried to cook up alternatives in our small ward space. That being said, we didn't actually have any stove or fireplace to work with. Did this stop my friends? No, of course it didn't. I personally didn't have much of an appetite, but it was a joy to watch them cook up something delicious under such limited circumstances. We had an old *samovar*[13] to make tea with. Do you think we used it only for brewing tea? Of course not. The steam from the samovar top was our one and only source to cook food. They would make paninis by placing the pieces of bread and cheese between two flat pot lids and cooking them over the heat of the steaming water. What's even more interesting, they would cook up *menemen* or even stir-fry, even soups and vegetable dishes. These interesting ventures sometimes took hours, but it always produced delicious results.

Living with limited means was our new lifestyle now... Having limited means opened up one's imagination in brand-new ways... We had friends who turned metal

---

13 A *samovar* is a metal container traditionally used to boil water and brew tea.

clothes hangers into knitting needles and knitted beautiful things. Because scissors were not allowed in the ward, some friends used a razor blade to cut and mend their clothes. They used a nail clipper to repair different odds and ends. The joy and energy radiating from them filled me with new strength and energy as well, so much so that I would sometimes forget where we actually were. Even if I forgot, my illness certainly did not. Sometimes, my chest would tighten up so badly that I couldn't move a muscle. If I happened to walk a bit around the courtyard, my knees would start shaking. When I had no other choice than to let myself down on the ice-cold concrete, I would merely smile trying to avert the concerned looks from my friends.

I kept writing requests to be sent to the hospital again. With each new day, Lupus was taking over more and more of my body. Swelling and lumps were emerging throughout my body, and these lumps caused pain. Because my illness was a blood disorder it was everywhere, but at the same time nowhere. Only very detailed bloodwork and tests could reveal where the true damage to the tissue was, which meant that I could find myself suffering from a heart attack or some other organ failure at any moment. Yet, though everything seemed to be getting worse and worse, for some reason, the thought of death never occurred to me. I don't think anyone can actually sense that they're going to die, unless the Lord specifically sends you that feeling. Death was so present and yet so distant from life itself. Like a butterfly, fluttering out of nowhere and silently settling on your shoulder... I think the only way to be prepared for it would be to never forget its presence.

As time wore on, even regular everyday tasks left me gasping for breath. Trying to climb the stairs to the second floor of the ward had become like torture. There were even some mornings when the guard on duty had to "count" me from my bed. Even their reprimands and threats couldn't get me up out of my bed on those days. My friends couldn't help themselves and would argue with the guards about how sick I was and how I wasn't being given the proper care, while I was mostly silent. They asked how I could stay so calm and not give them a piece of my mind, yet they already knew the answer. Those guards' actions were a display of their own characters. There was no need to beat myself up anymore because I had not done anything that would put me to shame in front of my Lord. Because no matter what I did, no matter how much I fussed and flittered, I could not break away from what was destined to be. I believed in the fact that my Lord knew me and saw me, and how despite all my efforts and struggles I could not break free from the chain of obstacles set before me. He knew it all, and this was all part of a test. It was obvious what needed to be done at this moment. I would keep on making the effort to obtain the healthcare I needed while also keeping faithful in my servanthood to my Lord. When it came to the perpetrators of all this aggression, the Lord of us all would have the final word. And what importance would my word carry next to His? Even if they absolutely deserved it, I was not of a character that would insult any other being. Trying to speak to and get a message across to some people was only a waste of resources, and I did not have the strength for that anymore. I was calm and collected from my core, and it bode me well.

I know I'll never be able to return the favor to any of my ward friends for all they did for me. Even though I insisted many times over, they refused to let me take on any cleaning or cooking duty in the ward. I think one other thing that really struck their compassion chord towards me was the fact that, except for one older brother, all my family members were so far away. Some saw me as their daughter, some saw me as their sister; they fussed over me and coddled me with compassion and great care. Yes, I may have fallen captive to a group of demons, but I was here together with these wonderful women.

I was grateful.

As believers, we were individuals who were already used to living a disciplined life, even during our days of freedom. Worship, prayer, waking up early, acquiring knowledge and eating little were already part of our lifestyle. Given the circumstances we had found ourselves in, we did the best we could to keep up with our normal routines. Like everything else, the books we had were also very limited. For instance, a friend and I would take turns reading from the one copy of the Holy Qur'an that we had on hand. I would pray to my Lord for forgiveness and for the recovery of my health.

These were the days we came to understand just how illusive this world really was, how none of the things we thought we owned actually belonged to us. They had stripped us of all our possessions, our assets, our freedom, but, worst of all, our reputation and dignity. Our days of freedom felt like they had never been. Were a person not to have a strong faith in the Afterlife, these losses would be completely unbearable. As if losing our jobs were not already enough, our diplomas were declared null and void as well. But no matter who did what injustice to us and how they did it, what was essentially happening was this: our Lord was taking back the trusts He had entrusted us with, to use during this short life. He was taking them back before the ultimate end which awaited us, our death.

When looking back at the things that had happened to me, I saw that the words of *Bediuzzaman*[14] resonated in me: *"Even when a tyrant oppresses, the Divine Destiny executes Justice."* At times, my Lord would send His message even through the hands of evil people, and then He would turn around and give them what they also deserved. I would think about what my Lord would want from me, where He would want me to stand, and I would strive to stand there. Still, I was only human, and I needed the assurance that those who tried to crush us like insects would one day have to answer for all they did. As I thought about the Afterlife, I would feel both fear and relief all at once.

---

14 See footnote 6 on page 44.

Manifesting the prayers into reality

You know how sometimes you'll be in the middle of winter, but then you'll be blessed with a day that feels like it's summer again, and you'll be surprised but so happy and joyful... Such was the case of us Hizmet volunteers, living a life behind iron bars. Here we were, standing in the middle of an icy cold winter, but in our hearts and minds we carried the warmth and sweet memories of our days of summer spent with Hizmet. Our spiritual world blossomed with overflowing joy and excitement. A non-stop 24-hour cycle of Qur'an recitation and continuous prayers and worship filled our living space with a divine ambiance. Because we were free of worldly chores and preoccupations like housework, child care, work life, etc. our minds and hearts had found a new kind of clarity and sharpness. It sometimes felt to me like we had specially been chosen to gather here like this. It was like we needed to experience it all... It was like a hand had reached down and picked us up as we were racing at full gallop after worldly worries and endeavors to remind us, "Are you certain you're headed in the right direction?" I was certain now. We could see what it was that we truly needed. All of us were filled with such passion towards worship. As I looked around at us, I likened it to the way a person heartily gulps down water after being stranded in the desert for a long period of time. Prisons are known to be the dwelling place of problematic and chaotic souls, a place where peace and tranquility is probably the last thing you will find. For us, it turned out to be the opposite. Even the guards who despised us could not help but comment on it from time to time. Fights, theft, chaos, riots -- there was none of it. A quiet calmness spread over our ward. Whenever some meaningless shriek made its way to our ears from other wards filled with perpetrators of petty crimes, chills would run up and down my spine, and I would turn to the spiritual environment of our own ward to find comfort in the peace and safety I felt there. All in all, I can say that I wasn't complaining too much about being locked in there. If I had been truly healthy, I could have very well gone on doing my worship, keeping quiet and serving the sentence of a crime I did not commit. But unfortunately, I was not healthy… at all.

One evening as we were sitting around and chatting, I felt dizzy like I could faint any minute. I leaped up and decided to try my luck that night. "I'm not feeling good, I'll tell them to take me to a doctor," I said. My friends were taken by surprise. "At this hour?" they asked. "Yes," I replied, "I'm certain my illness is at its worst right now." I walked over and pressed hard on the call button. As the guards traipsed in, I told them I wanted to be taken to a doctor, that I was feeling very ill. Grumbling, they took me out. However, our journey did not last long. There was a space in the middle of the building that we had named "the aquarium", they sat me down there. "The aquarium" was a section used by the guards and other employees. Surrounded by clear glass windows, there was no enclosed areas in it, which is why we had named it the aquarium. They sat me there for quite a long time. An ambulance arrived, they measured my blood pressure, and blew me off with a simple, "There's nothing wrong with you; you're probably a bit distressed." I told them about my chronic illness and about the fact that I hadn't been able to take any of my medication. I said, "My illness is getting worse and worse. I need to have bloodwork done. I'm asking you to please take me to a hospital." But no matter what I said to them it was all in vain. I was taken back to the ward. It was yet another one of my failed attempts to get help.

What you said or did was of no importance in there. Your right to speak was only about as much as an unwanted pest that happened to come out of a hole somewhere. And if you happened to get on the nerves of any one of them, they could very well squish you and even get promoted for it.

Nonetheless, I refused to lose hope. Even if in their

eyes we were nothing but insects, God Almighty was our Protector and Master. He certainly would listen and respond to us. Even the words and wishes that happened to come out in a moment of pain, my Lord would hear it all... I remember wishing for those who refused to believe that I really was ill, who kept treating me like I was a liar; I remember wishing that they too would get acquainted with this illness of mine. My friends themselves are witnesses that the wish of mine truly found its place. There was one other wish that had trickled from my lips, and my Lord had accepted that one as well. One night when we were chatting and pouring out our heart's griefs to one another, we spoke about the cruel and heartless treatment we had received from the judges and prosecutors, and I remarked, "I pray that my Lord saves me from this place without the need for a court trial, without having to face those heartless judges again." Those who had witnessed my prayer that night also witnessed my exit from that prison ward, without another court trial. They were there to witness how I took wings like a bird and was set free from the clutches of those tyrants.

Why did I not want another court trial? The genocide band encircling us was already getting tighter and tighter by the minute. The rule of law did not function for those like me. I hadn't even been able to find a lawyer to represent me. Among my ward friends, only a very few of them had actually been able to find good and reliable lawyers to represent them. Being the lawyer of a FETO (!) member was not the popular thing to be, as you can imagine. They were afraid to be labeled as FETO members themselves. Among the few who were willing to represent us were the blood-suckers asking for unreasonably large representation fees. And despite the large sums of money they received, they were still unwilling to put in a good fight for us. As for the ones appointed by the government, you can say they were pretty much invisible, an identity element so to speak. They carried the "attorney" title but due to the pressure on them and their own cowardice, they were merely acting as speakers for the prosecuting office and nothing more. In any event, there still was no indictment out there for me, and I had no money to throw out the window anyhow. Had ours been a normal country with a functioning legal system and had I had an honest lawyer, I would've been able to get a hold of my medication and my health report long ago. I could've even been released. Come to think of it, had that all been the case, this story would never have been written, would it?

Medicine delayed only makes the ailment worse
My brother was finally able to send me the weekly and daily medicines I needed to take. By then, a very painful and exhausting two months had passed by. When we saw that nothing was moving forward, he had gone directly to the pharmacy to purchase the medicine himself that normally needed to be prescribed by the rheumatologist. This was the only solution we could think of. It had been late, and it had been hard.

Upon returning to the ward, I filled up a glass of water. I opened up the package with trembling hands and took the medicine according to the dose when I had last taken it. The expectation was that it would give me some comfort. Unfortunately, it did not. I was laying down on my bed. About an hour or so later, I started feeling horrible. It felt like I was dying. "Something's happening to me," I said to my friends. It looked as if the medicine I hoped would be a cure for my ailment was instead fast-forwarding me to my end. Both my illness and its medicine required great caution and care. Had I made a terrible mistake in taking the dose I had used two months ago? But what else could I have done? I needed to have a specialist doctor reevaluate me according to my bloodwork and recalculate the dosage of the medicine I needed. Yet for that to happen, I needed to be able to reach a specialist doctor first. My status was as critical as ever, I was well aware of that. My vital organs could very well have been damaged, and I told my friends so as they all gathered around my bed. My intention was not to make them sad, but they needed to know. They were devastated. Some were crying. Others were cursing those who were responsible for my situation getting to this point.

Within the hierarchy of the prison system, the second-most responsible authority figure right after the prison warden is who we refer to as the "chief." In my last attempt to explain my situation, I had been trying to get the attention of this chief. Weeks ago, I had sent in a written request asking to meet with the chief. My request going all the way up to the chief and then getting back to me with a response etc. had taken quite a long period of time. So much so that I was still waiting for a response.

I have no idea how much time passed or did not pass after that. Well, the night and day of a person suffering and a person who's in good spirits is surely not the same. The nights are endless for the one who is suffering. Minutes can become hours, weeks can become years. Though my story spanned over a period of two months on the calendar, only my Lord knows how long it felt for me.

When I was finally able to meet with the chief, these were the words I spoke to him: "See here, this is the illness that I'm grappling with. The guards keep insulting me saying there's nothing wrong with me, but there is. My bloodwork at the hospital was not done properly; I was wronged incredibly and am suffering greatly as a result of it. I've just now started taking the medication I need, but it's too late and I'm seriously not well. If I end up dying, know that you will have to answer for it. Maybe not today, not right away. But one day, when the rule of law returns, all of this will come back to haunt you. I'm standing here, asking you for something that is my legal right. Please respect the law. I have to be admitted to a fully equipped hospital immediately."

The chief gave approval for me to be sent to a hospital. I had no strength left within me by this stage so I couldn't even rejoice at the news. Under normal circumstances, it would be my God-given right to seek treatment in a hospital. What a shame, here we were being subject to such inhumane treatment that we felt the need to rejoice when someone showed a normal human behavior. Yes, at last, I would finally be able to go to a hospital, but with all the procedures and protocols that needed to be followed, it would still take at least a week before I actually made it there. Like a never-ending story... the whole ordeal would have to start all over again. I would first have to go to the prison infirmary, they would have to notify the gendarmerie, the gendarmerie official would then have to set up an appointment with a doctor... At long last, my transfer to the Tarsus Public Hospital was finalized for the 25th of April. The only problem was that there was no Rheumatology Department - the department that would be treating my illness - at that hospital. Once again, I was going to have to go through the General Internal Medicine Department. I would first have to be seen by General Medicine and then be referred to a specialist. This would only mean more days of waiting.

The day of my appointment at the hospital was also the day I submitted a series of closed-envelope letters to several high officials regarding my right to healthcare which I had been denied for the past two months. The right to healthcare was the fundamental right of even a serial killer in prison and I had been denied the treatment I was so in need of. I learned about the closed-envelope petition right from the jurist friends in the ward. While the prison administration could open up and read an ordinary letter written by an inmate, letters specifically written as a closed-envelope letter were under legal protection. I was determined to file my complaints to the necessary institutions in the closed-envelope style because the prison administration was like a wolf shameless enough to devour the lamb and then insult the lamb for having tired his chin.

I wrote a petition of complaint to six different institutions (Prime Ministry Communications Center-BIMER, Presidential Communications Center-CIMER, Penitentiary Prosecutions Office, Ministry of Justice, The General Attorney Office, and the Institution of Human Rights). It may have been too late for me by then. So be it! But one day, when the rule of law returned from its forced exile, my petition would be waiting in the front row. These letters would be the painful cry I left behind. A cry that would forever ring in the ears of the tyrants who killed the rule of law.

How incredibly hard it had been to write those letters. I barely had the strength to hold a pencil and every so often I fell short of breath. As always, my friends rushed to my aide, and we finished writing the letters together. I handed the completed letters to the guards and from there headed to the hospital. As I was leaving, I said to my friends, "I'm going to ask the doctor to have me admitted to the hospital." I was exhausted, literally spent, with no more energy left in me. I could feel it, my body would not be able to hold on any longer. My friends all gathered to see me off and send me away with prayers. On the way to the hospital, I told the officer that I wanted to be admitted to the hospital, that I could die in the prison at any given minute if I returned. I wasn't threatening when I said that my death would cause a big problem for the entire prison administration. The officer's response was, "Not so easy to be admitted to the hospital." It turns out that a lot of inmates were making the same request just so they could get out of prison, even if only temporarily. One more hopeful moment fluttered away through my trembling fingers.

From that point on, I expected to fall into a coma any second. I was so weak, so helpless. In the end, the only thing that a human being truly does possess is the weakness, the incapability, is it not? My head fell to my chest, I bit my lips as tears fell down my face, and I prayed for forgiveness. I wasn't crying because I was going to die; I was crying because I hadn't been a dutiful servant to my Lord. If He would not forgive my sins, what was I to do?

Those who know me know that I don't easily complain or speak badly about anyone else. They had put an obstacle on every path I tried. For weeks they had pushed and shoved me around, hurt me excruciatingly. My dear Lord knew it all. "My Lord, it's over now. I tried, I did my best, but it didn't make a difference," I cried. It felt as if my whole being had been shredded to pieces and scattered all over the prison walls. Nevertheless, I could still forgive and forget it all. But the things they had done to all my Hizmet brothers and sisters, it tore away my heart. The cries of those innocent babies and children yearning for their mothers who were locked behind bars, it broke my heart into a thousand pieces. What pitiful creatures these people were, incapable of the slightest act of compassion and humanity, victimizing innocent children. It was an honor to be standing on the opposite side of the evil people whose worship was to their own egos and their hatred. What if I had a heart of stone just as they did, what if I had been standing right along with them applauding their tyranny? When you take compassion out of a person, what else is left but a carcass?

I could feel it, it was like death was standing right there, watching my every move. The thought of dying was not so scary anymore. The only thing that grieved me was that I had not fulfilled my duty of servanthood before my Lord. And also, the thought of my loved ones grieving after me. Other than that, actually, there was a secret joy bubbling inside me. Like it wasn't going to be scary at all, like I was going somewhere familiar... Like I would finally find peace...

If you're inside a compassionate heart, you are in the coziest of places...

Interestingly, the day I was finally able to go to the hospital after weeks of waiting turned out to be the day of open visitation in the prison which came around only once a month. How I longed to hold my brother in my embrace - the only family member still living in Turkey at that time - and catch up with him. I had a feeling that if I didn't get to see him today, I would not get a second chance. By the time I had my bloodwork done and got back from the hospital, open visitation hours were almost over. The guards actually having the grace to let me see my brother that day, I believe, was a special gift to me from my Lord. That visit would turn out to be the last time we saw each other in this world. When my brother saw how frail and weak I was, he was devastated. He asked me whether I was taking my medication. "Yes, I am," I said to him. I didn't have the heart to tell him that it was too late. I only smiled back at him. I told him to send my love and greetings to the whole family. I took the clean clothes that he had brought me.

When I woke up the next morning, I felt a bit better. I had gotten to see my brother the previous day and had an appointment at the rheumatology department. Towards noontime, my friends invited me over to the brunch they had set up in the courtyard. I didn't have the strength to make it down there though. I was hungry but didn't really feel like eating anything. I had really bad nausea and felt like I could lie in bed for days if they let me. I knew how happy it would make them to see me eat a few bites, so I didn't turn them down when they insisted. They took me by the arms and practically carried me to the table. As I listened to their cheery chitter-chatter, I ate a few bites with them. My dear sisters in fate were so happy to see me eating with them. Like a mother full of compassion for her child, they insisted that I "taste this" and "try that other one too." I tried my best to eat as much as I could not to hurt their feelings. If I didn't move aside and declare, "I'm stuffed," they would've continued with their coddling. "I'm not the same me anymore," were the thoughts running inside my head, "whatever I eat causes me suffering and nothing else." But I kept on smiling. I curled up my legs on the white plastic chair and listened to them chatter on. Their jokes and laughter comforted me like the singing of birds, but like I said, I did not have the strength to join in the conversation. I loved them all so dearly, like we had known each other for years, like we would see each other again in the future... Each and every one was a woman with a broken heart, having to fight an unexpected battle. None of them deserved to be here.

Each one had a story, a drama of her own. I prayed for each one of them, more than I prayed for myself. After a while, when they saw how tired I was, that I couldn't even hold up my head, they helped me to my bed so I could rest.

I walked with tiny steps, taking breaks in between as I climbed up the stairs and lay down on my bed. I was half-faint…so weak I didn't even have the strength to fret. It felt a little like my soul was at ease somehow, like the peace of having accepted my situation had been draped over me. As I watched from afar the fluster of my friends waiting before me and monitoring me from the sides, I was swimming in a sea of calm. I smiled back at my friends who kept coming back and forth, asking me, "Are you in any pain?" Even if I was in pain, I was not aware of it. I don't know how much time passed before I started shaking. One of my friends who was praying by my side started speaking to me, her voice sounded like it was coming from far away. "Look at her, her hands are ice-cold, but her head is burning up," she cried. Could a person burn up and be freezing cold at the same time? I was learning the answer firsthand. I was sweating cold, icy chills, but the inside of my head was burning hot. I could feel them trying to measure my blood pressure, their screams and their sobs were the last thing I heard as a hand reached down and pulled my consciousness far away. My head was spinning like I was being sucked into a vortex. I was losing myself in the midst of pitch-black darkness.

Minutes later I came to myself as my convulsions were starting to ease down. I had thrown up everything I had eaten at brunch. I felt so embarrassed to have caused so much trouble for my friends who were fluttering about me like delicate butterflies. They were cleaning me up. They had screamed and hollered for someone to come help, and when the guards finally came, the first thing they asked was, "What's the matter, who's fighting?" I guess that was the only thing that came to their mind since that's what you expect to happen in a prison cell, people fighting and hurting each other, right? "That's it, we're sick and tired of this," the guards were saying. They didn't want to have to deal with taking me to the hospital or the infirmary again. My friends were arguing with them, trying to convince them.

When they saw that my friends weren't backing down, they had finally grumbled, "All right, bring her over." But how were they supposed to get me down from the second floor? So they had asked for a stretcher. "What do you mean a stretcher?! Bring her somehow!" they scolded with indignation. Even a stretcher was seen as too much for us. Not wanting to risk the guards changing their minds, my friends carried me down from the second floor, holding me like a baby, snug in their arms. Here I was in cold sweats being carried to the door of this hole of oppression and seated in a wheelchair. After 10-15 meters, my friends carried me up in their arms again to the prison infirmary on the second floor. They had called the 112 Emergency Service. It felt like I was a dreaded chore everyone was trying to push on to another. I tried to explain my situation to the health officers hovering over me to assess the situation. Either I couldn't choose the correct words or their ears were elsewhere. They ended up diagnosing me with the flu, connecting an IV tube to my arm, and returning me back to the ward when they were done.

Shouldn't I at least have been kept under observation for one night? Bringing me back to the prison ward while my blood pressure was too imbalanced to even be measured, while I was unable to walk on my own, while I was practically in a half-coma…was this not blatant murder? I was a victim of cold-blooded murder. And not just once; I was murdered over and over, time and time again, relentlessly and in cold blood. I have countless daggers stabbed in my back. It was the government who stabbed the first dagger, labeling innocent people as terrorists, people who hadn't violated a single law or held a single weapon in their entire lives…Then it was the people, the people who ruthlessly applauded this slander... From the judge to the prosecutor, from the doctors to the prison guards, there are countless daggers both from neglect and intent, countless daggers stabbed on my back. And I was neither the first nor the last victim of the monsters whose eyes were infested with a passion for blood, a passion that was disguised as saving the country…the monsters were just covering up their evil and corrupt ways under the facade of a sacred calling.

Take me by the hand o death, take me to a faraway place...

When I was brought back to the ward, the guards didn't trouble themselves with coming inside and settling me in. Instead, it was my friends who carried me up to my bed in their arms. They were furious that I had been sent back like this. After I had left, they had changed the sheets I threw up in. They settled me back into my bed like a mother full of compassion taking care of her beloved child. I had been such a burden on them. I wanted to apologize to each and every one for all the disturbance I caused. I saw them weeping secretly, trying to hide it from me. I, on the other hand, was calm as ever. They held my hands tight and assured me that everything would be okay. I pray that God Almighty holds their hands when they need it most. One of them asked me once again, "Are you in pain Halime?" Like I told her, no, I am grateful to my Lord that I wasn't in any pain. Other than exhaustion and nausea, I didn't feel any other discomfort. My answer seemed to bring comfort to her as well.

The illness was taking over me, one bout after another. As my friends fluttered around me, wanting to help me however they could, I was being hit by death attacks. Yet, if you asked the guards about me, they would say I was fit as a fiddle. It felt like I was constantly being scolded by the guards because I was not dying quietly. It was like we were living inside a tragicomical movie. I would faint or be going through an attack, my friends would call the guards, they would take me some place, I would be set up with an IV or a painkiller, and I would be brought back to my prison ward. Like a joke, but a horrendous one, a deadly one…

My friends never once left my side, not for an instant. They took turns reading from the Qur'an by my side as they listened for my pulse and checked up on me. They too had accepted the fact that neither the doctor nor the hospital would reach out a hand to me, and they were holding on to prayers and worship, praying for my well-being.

We were nearing the end of April. The world was awakening to springtime, whereas I was left in the winter cold, shivering and shaking. A few hours later, another attack hit me, and as my body tensed up I felt disconnected from the world once again. It was like there was something inside me that was bursting to get out, trying to force its way out of my nerves and veins, fighting against me. I couldn't hear the sobs of my friends who were gathered all around me. I was unconscious. Once again, they took me in their arms, down to the door of the ward to hand me over to the guards. Had I the strength to open my mouth and speak, I would have said to them, "Please don't give me to those people again. I don't want a hospital or a doctor anymore, I want to give my last breath in peace, here with you." I felt at home here with my friends. I would forever remain indebted to them. Their smiling faces had enlightened this dungeon for me, and I had never felt like a stranger among them. It felt as though we had gathered here for a spiritual retreat, making the most of our days and nights. Four of my friends had weaved their hands together to make a chair for me as they carried me down. I tried hard to open up my eyes; I remember it like a dream. Tears were streaking down some of their faces, others were trying to hide their sobs. As the guards took me away in a wheelchair, I looked up with a weak smile to bid farewell...

It was about 2 am in the middle of the night when I was brought to the hospital emergency service. I was surrounded by white walls, white curtains...a quick examination, and another IV tube... I did not want to see any IV tube, medicine or doctor ever again. I did not want to see the gendarmerie officers following my every step. The only thing I wanted was for them to leave me be. When the IV was finished, they put me in the wheelchair and took me to the prison vehicle. And here we were, back at the ward. I was beyond exhausted from being thrown back and forth like a ping-pong ball. It was sickening the way they treated me as if I were a piece of trash standing in their path that they could just kick around as they pleased.

While we made our way back, my dear friends had put together a floor bed on the first floor of the ward for me. Climbing the stairs up and down was getting really hard on all of us. They settled me down in my new bed. I thanked them with a frail voice. They were like my true blood sisters, going through all the troubles for me. Tribulations are surely nothing to rejoice over, but I felt blessed to have met these wonderful human beings. They did not leave me alone for a second. If only I was able to erase the sadness they felt for me from their eyes. They looked out for my every need, from whether I wanted to drink a glass of water to changing me into a fresh set of clothes when I got drenched in sweat.

On Friday night, April 27, after another attack that left me passed out, my friends had called the guards to have me again taken to the hospital. It was 12:24 am…at an hour when most of the people behind the prison walls were asleep at their homes in their warm beds, I was lying on a floor-bed which was spread across the cold hard concrete of the prison floor, sweating blood and fighting for my life. As I started coming to myself and realized they were taking me out of my bed, I turned to my friends and barely made out a whisper, telling them I did not want to go. I was determined not to go, I did not want anything to do with a hospital or a doctor anymore. I did not want to move an inch from where I was. All I wanted was to rest in my bed quietly, in peace. My friends, however, were begging both me and the guards, insisting that it would be best for me to go to the hospital. Had I been able to resist the pleading of my friends, I would never have gone back to that cold hospital infested with ruthless doctors. The only reason I accepted was because I could not bring myself to say "No" to these kind souls who tried so hard to hide their tears from me. This turned out to be the last time I saw them!

The hospital I had not been able to go to for treatment turned out to be the hospital I was taken to, to die. They had succeeded in crashing down my world over me. Let their world devour them up and spit them out! A sick woman, too weak to even take a step, and I was escorted into the hospital vehicle completely surrounded by four gendarmerie officers and a sour-faced guard. The doors were locked behind us, and there was another inmate in there with me. Here I was, in the middle of the night, away from my home and my loved ones, stranded between these people who treated me like a vicious enemy, on my last ride... handcuffed, as if I had the strength to even attempt an escape…

When the other patients waiting in the emergency waiting room saw us walking in with gendarmerie officers surrounding us, they stepped aside and cleared a path. It was the same story every time we came to the hospital, yet it never got any easier, being treated like I was stricken with the plague. After being defamed as coup conspirators, the people had all turned against us. We felt it in our veins; what a burning venom slander and defamation could be. Yes, the government was constantly defaming and throwing dirt at us since we have not bowed down to its will; that would be the nature of their own malice. But what about the ordinary people on the street? They had seen nothing but goodness and grace from the Hizmet people around them, yet they stood and watched us as we walked before them in handcuffs like they were watching a parade of criminals. Seriously, how could a person become a traitor, a terrorist by only depositing money into a bank or being a subscriber to a newspaper? What was this total eclipse of sense and understanding?

The emergency doctor did a quick check-up and said I could go. I held on to the walls as I exited the room. I didn't ask, and they didn't say anything about any treatment etc. I'm assuming that the doctor thought I was being delusional again. Once the other inmate was finished, we would be going back to the prison. At this point, I didn't really care anymore. Out in the corridor, the gendarmerie officer motioned for me to sit on a bench. As I sat down, it felt like I was putting down the period at the end of the last sentence of the short story of my life. I felt all alone and helpless in the middle of an endless vacuum. "What did or did I not do to deserve all this?" was a question I asked myself over and over so many times. Each time, I found myself at the same answer. God Almighty knew the truth...

The silence of the night was being accompanied by the humming of the fluorescent lamps overhead. The gendarmerie officers were standing by my side. Slowly and softly, I rested my head on the shoulder of the other inmate we had come here with. She wasn't from our ward. I didn't know her at all. She said nothing and let me lay my head down on her shoulder. I was reciting some prayers I knew by heart as I slowly closed my eyes.

It was here, in this corridor, that my story would come to an end. Not long after, I don't know if it was the lights that went out or my eyes that went blind, but everything went dark. The thread that held me tied to my body slowly broke off... As my head dropped off her shoulder, the woman started screaming. As she jumped off her seat, the rest of my body toppled down over the bench. So I left myself behind. Like an empty cocoon, my dried-up body was left behind, just lying there. The soldiers called for a stretcher and the nurses rushed it over… the stretcher they had denied me when I was still alive. They quickly transferred my body to the stretcher and rushed it to the emergency room. Meanwhile, having completed its duty, my heart had stopped beating.

My name is Halime. On April 28, 2018, at 03:10 am, I gave my last breath. They murdered me. Neglect, ill intention, and persecution joined hand-in-hand and they succeeded in murdering me. From the judge to the prosecutor and all others who supported the hatred propagated by the Erdogan government, there are so many people who are responsible for my death. I was a victim of the genocide directed towards the volunteers of the Hizmet movement. They were going to write cardiac arrest on my death papers. What they should've written was… **murder**! A slow and silent one, slyly and savagely. The blood-thirsty murderers broke me down piece by piece, day by day…

They will try to change the reports, the statements, and the facts. They will try to evade taking responsibility. But everyone knows that I was in fact murdered.

Those whose hearts have darkened will be proud of their accomplishment. They will take pride in erasing one more "terrorist" off the face of the Earth. "She was a traitor!" they will say.

No matter what they say, what they don't yet realize is that their conscience will never be convinced that they did something good.

No matter how hard they scrub, my blood will not wash off their hands.

One day, these murderers who chose to lynch us for the crimes we had not committed will understand that "terror" was the very thing that they themselves had committed.

And they will face the Divine Justice!

They will witness that the Divine Justice does not operate on bribery!

They will see clearly that it stands with the rightful and not with the powerful!

Have no doubt!

When that day comes… I will be there!

NOTES

1- This story was written in light of information gathered from official documents, as well as a compilation of the accounts of Halime Gülsu's immediate family and prison mates.

2- An interesting anecdote from Halime Gülsu's prison mates: Soon after Halime's death, during a meeting with the inmates, the Prison Director complained about having been tied up at the hospital for a week, saying, "Damn those doctors! My wife has been sick for a whole week and they still haven't been able to make a diagnosis!" A week later, a diagnosis was made: Systemic Lupus Erythematosus, or just LUPUS. This was the same disease that was the cause of death of Halime.

3- During her life, Halime Gülsu had dedicated herself to helping those who were in difficult situations or in need of help of some kind. In the end, even her death ended up being a means of helping others. Following her death, Mersin Tarsus Department of Corrections, infamous for having the highest record of human rights violations, took steps to alleviate their harsh treatment and persecution of their convicts. Some of the rights of inmates who were Hizmet volunteers were reinstated.

4- Shortly before her death, using her legal right to do so, Halime Gülsu wrote a closed-envelope letter to six different institutions (Prime Ministry Communications Center-BIMER, Presidential Communications Center-CIMER, Penitentiary Prosecutions Office, Ministry of Justice, The General Attorney Office, and the Institution of Human Rights) and submitted them to be sent out. In her letter, she described the nature of her illness, talked about how her right to receive necessary treatment was denied and described the chain of neglect and abuse she was subject to. The letters were submitted to the prison guard with her prison-mates present as eyewitnesses. Whether or not these letters were in fact delivered to the intended addresses is still, to this date, uncertain. Below is the letter she wrote:

Halime Gülsu's Letter

To the corresponding government office,

On February 20, 2018, I was taken into custody by police officers of the Mersin Police Headquarters, Anti-Terror Branch Office, from my home address in Mersin. I was taken by surprise and was rushed out of my home with no previous warning, which resulted in me just barely being able to take only what was left of the medicine I used daily for my chronic illness known by the name Systemic LUPUS. Because I was rushed and flustered, I didn't have the opportunity to call up my family to inform them that I was almost out of my medicine and that I needed them to bring me a new supply immediately. What's worse, my other medicine which is the main medicine that I had to use weekly, had gotten left behind.

Systemic LUPUS Erythematosus is a condition in which the body's immune system is unable to recognize its own body tissue and starts attacking itself as though it were a foreign matter. The body produces an excessive amount of antibodies (white blood cells) and the immune system starts slowly killing itself. This abnormality initially brings about a sudden drop in blood pressure, followed by joint pains, exhaustion, fatigue, and weakness to the point where a person is unable to sustain even the basic functionality of life on their own. Following a diagnosis, a medical treatment plan is devised, and there are specific medications needed to be taken both on a weekly and daily basis. The illness must be under constant monitoring by a specialist doctor in which the active ingredient in the medication as well as the prescribed dosages must be reevaluated and adjusted according to the results of periodic bloodwork and examinations. This unique illness can only be monitored and treated by a specialist rheumatology doctor. What's more, because the body's natural production of antibodies (white blood cells) are suppressed as part of the treatment of the illness, being exposed to the bacteria and viruses present in the outside world poses a great risk to the patient. The patient thus would need to be in a sterile environment and be under constant monitoring. The treatment of this illness requires specific procedures and is a critical process.

For 15 years, I have been a Systemic LUPUS patient. After undergoing a long and tiring process, my illness had finally been taken under control and was in an inactive state. Yet, I was still following a strict medical treatment plan. However, as of the day I was taken under custody, I was only able to continue taking my daily medication. I was unable to take the treatment's main medication, my weekly medication, because the police had not notified my family of my whereabouts. The police officers had me sign a document stating that they had notified my family, but at a much later date, after I had been officially arrested and sent to jail, during a visit with my brother, I learned from him that no one had called to notify him of anything and that he was not made aware of the problem with my medication. While under custody for over a week, I was denied any form of communication, even a written note, and it was because of the police officers there that the medication I needed never reached me. While under custody, I was unable to take two doses of my weekly medication--two weeks without the main medication-- despite the fact that the medication was sitting there in my home.

During the court trial held at the Mersin 4th Criminal Court of Peace, in which I was arrested, neither the public attorney nor the appointed judge took any sort of action regarding my illness. I was arrested and sent to the Tarsus Closed Prison for Women. After being transferred there, I ran out of my daily medication and I have still not been able to take my weekly medication. Per the regulations of the prison, I wrote numerous petitions and letters with the inscription "Urgent" on top requesting an appointment with the prison infirmary doctor. I wrote so many petitions that I lost count, but none of my petitions received a response and I was not allowed up to the infirmary. About a month after my initial apprehension, including the time spent in custody and official arrest, I was finally taken to the Tarsus Public Hospital General Internal Medicine Department. I spoke to the doctor about my illness. I requested that all necessary bloodwork be carried out. However, I learned much later that they had only checked my hemogram, liver enzyme, TSH and ferritin numbers whereas the essential tests looking for the anti-DSDNA, C3, C4 and ANA numbers had not been worked up at all. Meanwhile, because the Anti-Terror Branch Office had lost the health report in which my illness was documented, and because my brother had never been notified of the situation, neither the prison infirmary doctor nor any responsible authority took any kind of action towards the treatment of my illness. Because the general medicine doctor had ordered incomplete bloodwork and because the essential tests necessary in detecting my illness were not conducted, the doctor informed the prison officers that I was in good health. With that, the prison infirmary doctor spoke to me, saying, "It turns out that there's nothing wrong with you." In response, I wrote a petition requesting to see the chief director of the prison. The director listened to my plea and gave orders to the infirmary doctor to have me referred to the Rheumatology department at the hospital. Finally, after having the chance to speak with my brother during a non-contact visit, I asked him to bring me my medication and health report. It took a week's time for the things I asked for to reach me. In total, it had been two months that I had been left without being able to take my medication.

During this time period, my illness had relapsed. Exhaustion, fatigue, muscle and joint pains, they all started back up again. To add to that, I suffered from nausea as well. I wrote another petition to the prison infirmary doctor, and again I was referred to the general medicine department at the hospital. Because there was no rheumatology department at Tarsus Public Hospital, I was again taken to the general medicine department. When I explained my situation to the doctor, the doctor said my illness could have relapsed and sent in a referral to the City Hospital rheumatology department. As of April 23, 2018, I have still not been taken to the rheumatology department.

Though I've been taking my medication after finally receiving it, I am not getting any better. Because the nature of the illness already makes it very difficult to treat in terms of procedures and the process of treatment, the use of medicine and the process of healing or recovery are not always directly proportional. For this reason, I spoke to the responsible authority figures in the prison regarding the need for new bloodwork tests to detect the specific values in my blood that were not where they should be. On April 20, 2018, an ambulance arrived from 112 Emergency Services. Despite the fact that I explained my unique situation to the responsible emergency persons, the only thing they did was take measurements of my blood pressure and pulse and send me back to my prison ward with the words, "God-willing, nothing bad shall happen." Because my illness does not produce an outwardly/physically apparent effect, the guards at the prison assume that I am lying and are constantly reprimanding me. My illness is serious to the extreme and can certainly end in death. Therefore, I hereby demand that the necessary procedures be initiated against all responsible persons holding a certain position and/or duty in the institutions of Mersin Police Headquarters (Anti-Terror Branch Office), Tarsus Closed Prison for Women, and Tarsus Public Hospital, who have neglected, delayed or failed to act on/according to their duties and responsibilities, with regards to the events mentioned within this petition, beginning with the day I was taken under custody and leading up to the present day in which I am writing this petition as a prisoner at Tarsus Closed

Prison for Women.

My final requests are that necessary legal actions regarding the aforementioned events be initiated on the part of your office, and any documentation records and date of actions related to this petition be delivered to my attention through responsible incumbents appointed by the Head Office of the Tarsus Closed Prison for Women. Let it be known that it is my constitutional right to be notified of the necessary information regarding the legal actions taken. In the event that the said information is withheld from me, my legal rights are being fully reserved.

Kindly submitted for necessary action.

Halime Gülsu

April 24, 2018

Closed Prison for Women, A-7 Tarsus/MERSİN

PHOTOS

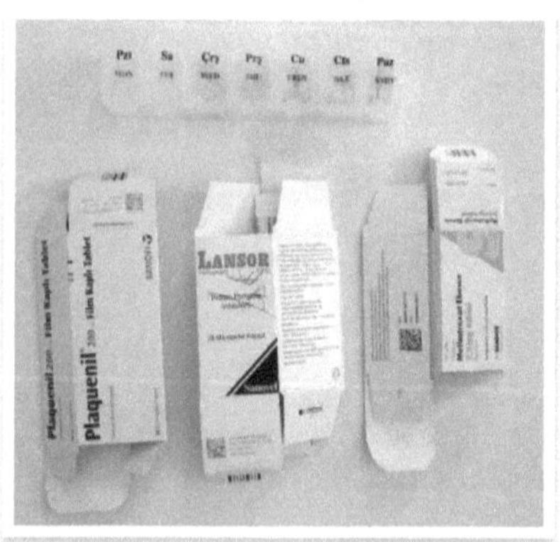

بسم الله الرحمن الرحيم
HALİME GÜLSU
Ruhuna Fatiha
D. 03.10.1984 - Ö. 28.4.2018

HALİME GÜLSU
28.04.2018
TENKIL
MUSEUM

REPORT ON HALİME GÜLSU

MAZLUMDER[15]
Adana Branch

May17, 2019

"We are for the oppressed, against the oppressor
No matter who they are"

The Association for Human Rights and
Solidarity for the Oppressed

---

15 Abbreviation in Turkish for "The Association for Human Rights and
Solidarity for the Oppressed"

PREFACE

O you who believe! Stand out firmly for justice, as witnesses to Allah, even as against yourselves, or your parents, or your kin, and whether it be (against) rich or poor; for Allah is nearer to both (than you are). Follow not (personal) inclination, so that you can act justly. If you distort or decline to do justice, know that Allah is well aware of all that you do.

(Quran, Chapter Nisa, verse 135)

O you who believe! Stand out firmly for Allah and be just witnesses and let not the hatred of others to you make you swerve to wrong and depart from justice. Be just; that is nearer to righteousness. And fear Allah; surely Allah is well-acquainted with all that you do.

(Quran, Chapter Maidah, verse 8)

The "right to life" is a fundamental human right. In this context, while public officials perform their duties, they are obliged to pay maximum attention to human rights. One of MAZLUMDER's missions is to observe the violations of rights and to share them with the public if necessary.

After the death of Halime Gülsu in prison, many allegations took place in the press and social media. To investigate these allegations, Mazlumder Adana Branch established a monitoring committee consisting of Mazlumder Adana Branch President Attorney Mehmet Ali Onal, Mazlumder Deputy Head Orhan Goktas and Mazlumder Adana Branch Deputy Head Attorney Ali Caldir.

This report, which is prepared by the Mazlumder Adana Branch, is a result of the observations and examinations made by this monitoring committee, with the support of other members of the Mazlumder Adana Branch, especially the physician members.

A. PURPOSE

Regarding the alleged violation of Halime Gülsu's right to life, to prepare a report as a result of the related observations and examinations.

B. EVENT SUBJECT TO THE REPORT

Halime Gülsu was detained on February 20, 2018 by an operation carried out by the Mersin Anti-Terror Branch Office, with the accusation of FETO/PDY organization membership. After staying in custody for 12 days, Mersin Chief Prosecutor's Office asked her to be arrested with the claim of being a member of a terrorist organization. As a result, on March 3, 2018 she was arrested by the Mersin Peace Court. Allegedly, while in prison, her medication was not given to her fully and in a timely manner, and she was not provided a medical treatment, and consequently Halime Gülsu died on April 27, 2018.

C. INSTITUTIONS AND PEOPLE INTERVIEWED

Upon the allegations in the press and social media regarding the death of Halime **Gülsu** in prison, the monitoring committee conducted separate interviews with Halime Gülsu's older brother Sinan Gülsu, the officers in the administration of the Tarsus Closed Prison for Women, and a woman who stayed with Halime Gülsu together in the police custody and then in the same prison ward. That woman requested that her name be kept confidential.

Our committee requested to meet with prison doctor as well as the personnel and doctors in the Mersin City Hospital and Tarsus State Hospital, where Halime Gülsu was taken several times during her stay in prison. However, we have not received a positive or negative response to our request and thus we couldn't talk to any of these doctors.

D. INTERVIEWS MADE

1. INTERVIEW WITH SİNAN GÜLSU, HALIME GÜLSU'S BROTHER

After the news about Halime Gülsu's death spread on the social media, the monitoring committee reached Halime

Gülsu's brother Sinan Gülsu by phone and requested an interview, in order to have first-hand information about the event. Upon the acceptance of the meeting request, an interview was held with Sinan Gülsu on January 25, 2019 at his workplace in Mersin. Our committee explained the reason for the meeting to Sinan Gülsu and his information about the allegations was sought.

His statements are as follows: "I am the brother of Halime Gülsu who lost her life while she was imprisoned in Tarsus Closed Prison for Women. My sister was diagnosed with SLE (Systemic Lupus Erythematosus) in 2003. Police officers of Mersin Anti-Terror Branch raided my sister's apartment at 6:10 am in the morning of February 20, 2018. I was totally unaware of where she was brought to and by whom. Later on, I learned that Mersin Anti-Terror Branch Office raided on that day simultaneously the houses of 24 individuals - including my sister - with the accusation of FETO/PDY terrorist organization membership. I was then called around 2:00 pm on that day by the Mersin Yenisehir District Police Department by phone and asked to bring her medicines. I picked up some of her medicines from the pharmacy and brought them to the police department along with her health report. Later, I was called again from the police department and more medicine were requested. I again delivered the requested drugs but not all of them, because I couldn't get hold of some of them. I could not visit my sister for 12 days while she was in custody, I was told that only her lawyer could meet with her. On March 3, 2018 a lawyer appointed by the Mersin Bar Association called me and said that my sister was arrested and sent to Tarsus Closed Prison for Women. On March 8, 2018 I was allowed to visit my sister in prison, and she told me that she was doing fine. During the visit, I asked her about the medicines. She told me that she met with the doctor in prison and told the doctor about her illness, however the doctor did not have any knowledge about her disease because he was not a specialist, and therefore he did not understand what my sister explained to him about her disease. Later, my sister was taken to a hospital but a doctor listened to her for a short while and then she was sent back to the prison. My sister reproached by saying that they didn't understand her situation."

Sinan Gülsu continued: "On March 15, 2018, in a visitation I held with my sister through glass partitions, my sister told me that her medicines were running out, her health report that I brought earlier was lost by the district police department, that she had difficulties to get her medicine and that I should bring all the medicine at home to her. I went to a doctor for the corresponding medicine to be prescribed, but since my sister appeared in prison, he did not prescribe any medicine. I went to the pharmacy to get the drugs, but due to some difficulties regarding the database system, I couldn't get them. I took a copy of her health report to the prison, and later she called me on the phone and said that her medicines arrived."

Sinan Gulsu continued: "On April 25, 2018 I had a contact visitation with my sister. She had lost so much weight, her skin was dry, her eyes turned yellow, and her physical appearance was extremely changed. She had difficulties speaking, her illness had progressed significantly. One day before my sister's death, I met with a woman who was recently released from the same prison and who was staying earlier in the same ward together with my sister. That woman told me that she witnessed the course of my sister's illness and the whole process she lived in prison, that my sister's situation was very critical and she was about to die. One day after this meeting, an officer from the prison called me and said that my sister passed away. My sister died because her medicine was not given her in a timely manner and because she was not provided a medical treatment."

Upon being asked, Sinan Gülsu stated that they could not afford to hire a lawyer for her sister due to lack of financial means.

2. INTERVIEW WITH THE OFFICIALS AND PERSONNEL OF THE TARSUS CLOSED PRISON FOR WOMEN

Our monitoring committee, having interviewed Halime Gülsu's brother, requested a meeting with the administration of the Tarsus Closed Prison for Women by sending an e-mail to the administration's e-mail address. Shortly after, the prison administration replied stating that they accepted our request of interview. The interview took place in the room of the prison warden and the prison warden Mazlum Ozalp, deputy wardens Demet Mat and Ahmet Hocamoglu, prison officer Osman Ince, infirmary officer Ali Ozkara attended the meeting along with the members of our committee. After a brief introduction about the purpose and activities of our association, our reason for this meeting is stated along with the allegations related to the cause of death of Halime Gülsu.

During the meeting, prison warden Mazlum Özalp said, "Halime Gülsu was held in our institution under arrest. I have been following the allegations in the press and the social media, but the truth is very different than what is alleged. Some people and the media is distorting the truth. The medications of Halime Gülsu were given to her, she was transferred to a hospital and all these were recorded. He stated that Halime Gülsu did not die in prison, but she died in Tarsus State Hospital. He continued saying that Halime Gülsu was taken to hospital 13-14 times, even on the day of her death, and that she died in the hospital. According to his statement, their institution is transparent and open to inspection, there are 65 FETO arrestees in their institution, no discrimination is made against these people, all the inmates in the prison are treated well, and the children and elderly are positively discriminated.

Our committee asked about the allegation that Halime Gülsu submitted an official complaint letter to the prison administration to be sent to the prosecutor's office. Although the letter was dated April 24, 2018 it was allegedly sent to the prosecutor's office only after the death of Halime Gülsu.

In response, prison warden Mazlum Ozalp said: "After the letter was delivered to us, we sent it to the prosecutor's office. According to the prison regulations, the letters of the inmates are collected by the guards on a specific day and delivered to us. If the letters are written to individuals, they are read by us. However, if the letter is written to an institution, it is not read. The letter of Halime Gülsu was submitted to a guard by her friends.

On another note, Halime Gülsu was arrested on March 3. She didn't have enough medication with her, sufficient only for one week. 32 days after her arrest, her medication was delivered. It is up to the physician that no medication was prescribed earlier, this has nothing to do with us. Also, if any kind of medication is delivered to the prison from outside, that medication is delivered to the inmate under the supervision of the prison doctor."

Health Officer Ali Ozkara said in response: "The prisoner arrived here on the weekend. Her medication was delivered on Monday, and we gave her medicines to her. On March 13, she was referred to a hospital with the diagnosis of SLE."

Deputy warden Demet Mat said in response: "I have been working here for the last four months. I was not here when she died."

The prison administration stated that Doctor Caglar Ozen, who was the prison doctor at the time of the death of Halime Gülsu, was on leave at the time of the interview. Apparently, he is not working in the Tarsus Closed Prison for Women anymore, but he is on duty in a T2 style prison. Despite our committee called him many times, it was not possible to get hold of him and to have a conversation.

3. INTERVIEW WITH THE PERSON WHO STAYED IN THE POLICE CUSTODY AND PRISON WARD TOGETHER WITH HALİME GÜLSU AND WHO REQUESTED HER NAME TO BE KEPT CONFIDENTIAL

Sinan Gülsu, the brother of Halime Gülsu, had mentioned during our interview that he had talked to a woman who had stayed in the police custody and prison ward together with his sister and who later was released from the prison. Our committee asked Sinan Gülsu to reach that person and ask her whether she would agree to meet with the members of our committee. She accepted our request but asked her identity to be kept confidential. After our committee guaranteed that her name to be kept confidential, the interview took place in March 2019, in a public place in Adana. We first introduced our organization and our works and then explained the reason of the interview and the allegations related to the death of Halime Gülsu.

In the interview, the person said: "On February 2, 2018 around 6 am, while I was at home, I was taken into custody by the police officers of Mersin Anti-Terror Branch Office. For the following 12 days, I stayed in a small detention room inside the Yenisehir District Police Department, together with six other persons. One of these persons was Halime Gülsu. The police officers who were in charge of the detention room were female and they were kind towards us, mostly. Halime was sick, she was using medication. She told us that she was supposed to take different types of medication, on a daily, weekly, and six-monthly basis. She told the police officers that she needed to take her medication and requested them to contact her family for her medication to be brought to the police station. Sometime later, she complained that some of her medications arrived, but not all of them. While in custody, we were not given any water to drink in the mornings, only juice. Water was given twice a day, half a liter around noon, another half a liter in the evening. We told to police officers that the amount of the water we were supplied was insufficient, we even asked whether we could purchase water, but our requests were not taken into account. Actually we were told by the police officers that we could drink tap water, and those of us who drank tap water soon started to have abdominal pain, diarrhea, etc. and eventually a doctor visited the detainees in the police station. Halime had to consume a lot of water due to her illness, but the water was limited and so the other people in the detention room shared their water with her. We stayed in that detention room for 12 days and after our statements were taken we were sent to the Peace Court and got arrested. When we were sent to the Tarsus Closed Prison for Women, Halime stayed in the temporary ward for 2 days. It was March 5, 2018 when we moved to another ward together. There, Halime explained her illness to me and said that she had been using medication for the last 16 years. She also told me that her health report was lost while we were in the custody, that she couldn't get her medication without her health report, that her prescribed medications were not delivered to her, and that the disease would relapse if she could not use her medication regularly. Halime was constantly sighing and breathing deeply in the ward, she was constantly tired and exhausted. She was frequently talking to the prison doctor and requesting to be referred to the hospital. She wanted to be seen by a rheumatology doctor, but the prison doctor did not understand her situation and referred her several times to the internal medicine department. Since she was seen by a doctor in the internal medicine department, her medications were not subscribed. Each time she was seen by a doctor in a hospital, she asked to be admitted to the hospital, but she was never admitted. In April, her medications were fully delivered to her, but she could not get better although she was using her medications. Upon her request, some bloodwork tests were performed but Halime said that some of the tests that she had requested were not done. While she was climbing the stairs to the second floor of the ward where the beds were located, Halime had to give a few rest breaks. Eventually, she could not climb the stairs by herself anymore, we had to support her by holding her arms and her waist. During the last 3-4 days before her death, Halime could not take care of her personal needs anymore, her close friends were helping here for her personal needs. Once, Halime lost her consciousness and had difficulty breathing since her tongue blocked her throat. The inmates around used a tablespoon to bring her tongue forward so that she could breathe again. On April 24, 2018 an ambulance came from the hospital, the health personnel measured Halime's blood pressure, they said that she was fine and didn't bring her to the hospital. We asked for a stretcher from the prison administration so that we could carry Halime between the first floor where the bathrooms were located and the second floor where the beds were located. No stretcher was provided. One week before her death, Halime decided to send letters to around 6-7 institutions about her illness and some complaints. Since Halime was exhausted, she didn't have the strength to write those letters, so several inmates wrote down what she said."

A member of our committee said that the letters

were dated April 24, 2018. Upon that, the person said: "I am absolutely sure that the letters were written one week before her death. Perhaps the dates were added later."

E. EXAMINATION OF DOCUMENTS

The documents which were used in the investigation (2018/5926) of the Tarsus Chief Public Prosecutor's Office have been examined, along with the statement records of Halime Gülsu which were obtained from Sinan Gülsu, the brother of Halime Gülsu.

As a result of the investigation, it has been observed that

– Halime Gülsu was taken into custody at Yenişehir District Police Department on February 20, 2018. Her statement was taken at Mersin Anti-Terror Branch Office on February 28, 2018. On the second page of that statement, she mentioned that "since 2003, she has been suffering from SLE" and on the third page she mentioned that "the disease has relapsed while she was working in a private school, and for that reason she had to quit her job."

– Within the scope of the investigation file (2017/63066) of the Mersin Chief Public Prosecutor's Office, Halime Gülsu gave a statement to the prosecutor's office on March 3, 2018 and mentioned the following: "I have been diagnosed with Systemic Lupus. It is a disease of the immune system. Regarding this, I have been receiving treatment and using medicine. I want all these to be taken into consideration."

– Halime Gülsu was arrested by the Mersin 4th Court of Peace on March 3, 2018, inquiry number 2018/294.

– A sheet of A4 paper, undated, with the names of some medications and a note written on it such as *"to be delivered upon doctor's examination"* was received on which there is a signature which our committee considers that it belongs to Halime Gülsu.

– On March 14, 2018 Halime Gülsu was examined by the family physician of the prison and was referred to the hospital with the "stated diagnosis of SLE."

– On March 16, 2018 Halime Gülsu was examined at Tarsus State Hospital Internal Medicine Polyclinic, where a blood sample is taken for analysis.

– On March 17, 2018 Halime Gülsu was referred to Tarsus State Hospital Emergency Polyclinic and examined.

– On March 26, 2018, the results of blood tests came out.

– On April 5, 2018 the medications, a paper showing

the list of the medications, and a copy of her medical report which were brought to the prison by her relative were delivered to Halime Gülsu for signature.

– On April 11, 2018 a prescription was issued by the prison doctor with the diagnosis of SLE and Halime Gülsu was referred to Tarsus State Hospital Internal Medicine Polyclinic.

– On April 16, 2018 after the examination performed at Tarsus State Hospital Internal Medicine Polyclinic, Halime Gülsu was referred to the Mersin City Hospital Rheumatology[16] Polyclinic.

– On April 20, 2018 the 112 Emergency Service was called to the prison and Halime Gülsu was examined, upon which a document was prepared with the following note on it: *"The patient's urgent referral to the required polyclinic is appropriate."*

– On April 25, 2018 Halime Gülsu was referred to the Mersin City Hospital Rheumatology Polyclinic and examined, upon which the patient was asked to be brought back again to the hospital together with the results of the tests made.

– On April 26, 2018 the 112 Emergency Service was

---

16 As of the referral date, there was no Rheumatology Polyclinic in the Tarsus State Hospital.

called to the prison and Halime Gülsu was examined, upon which she was referred to the Tarsus State Hospital Emergency Polyclinic and examined, upon which it was stated that the patient's examination by the Rheumatology Polyclinic was appropriate.

– On April 26, 2018, again, during the night, the 112 Emergency Service was called to the prison and Halime Gülsu was examined, upon which she was referred to the Tarsus State Hospital Emergency Polyclinic, which stated that the patient's examination by the Mersin City Hospital Rheumatology Polyclinic was appropriate.

– On April 27, 2018 prison administration handed over a notice letter (dated April 27, 2018 with the file number 2018/9272) to the Prison Gendarmerie Battalion Command officers, which was about the referral of Halime Gülsu to the Mersin City Hospital Rheumatology Polyclinic.

– On April 27, 2018 Halime Gülsu's condition got worsened during night hours; the 112 Emergency Service was called to the prison. After she was examined, she was referred to the Tarsus State Hospital Emergency Polyclinic with the diagnosis of SLE (Attack), with the complaint notice of "abdominal pain."

– On April 27, 2018 around 11:25 pm Halime

Gülsu was taken to the Tarsus State Hospital Emergency Service. After she was examined, she was discharged. While she was taken to the prison vehicle in front of the hospital entrance, her condition got worsened and she was brought back into the hospital.

– On April 28, 2018 around 12:24 am Halime Gülsu was taken into the Tarsus State Hospital. On April 28, 2018 around 3:10 am Halime Gülsu *"lost her life due to cardiac arrest related to SLE."*

F. EXAMINATION OF THE COMPLAINT LETTER THAT IS SENT BY HALİME GÜLSU TO PUBLIC INSTITUTIONS AND ORGANIZATIONS AND OTHER RELEVANT AUTHORITIES

The complaint letters that were written and signed by Halime GÜLSU and sent to many institutions (Prime Ministry Communications Center – BIMER, Ministry of Justice – General Directorate of Prisons and Detention Centers, Tarsus Public Prosecution Office, Tarsus Prison Prosecution Office) were got hold of in the investigation file. These letters were examined by our committee. They were dated April 24, 2018 and they had different handwriting types and styles, which suggest that they were written by different people. At the bottom of all the letters the name and signature of Halime GÜLSU were present. The signatures were similar to each other. The letters emphasized the events related to her illness and the severity and the course of her illness during the time period from the date of her detention until 4 days before the date of her death. It has been found out that although the letters were dated April 24, 2018, **they were recorded into the prison file system on May 5, 2018; after the death of Halime Gülsu on April 28, 2018.** Furthermore, it has been found out that the letter that was written to the Tarsus Public Prosecutor's Office was transferred to that office on August 11, 2018.

Upon examination of the complaint letter that Halime Gülsu wrote and signed on April 24, 2018 to be sent to the Tarsus Public Prosecution Office, it has been observed that:

– On February 20, 2018 she was taken into custody by police officers. Since the police rushed her out of her home, she was only able to take enough medicine for one week. Because she was rushed, she didn't have the opportunity to call up her family to inform them that she was almost out of her medicine and that she needed a new supply. One week after her detention, her daily medication was brought by her brother. Since she couldn't talk to her brother, she couldn't let him know about the main medication that she needed to use weekly. Although that main medication was at home, during her detention she couldn't use it for two consecutive weeks. Neither the public attorney nor the court of peace took any sort of action regarding her illness. She was arrested and sent to the Tarsus Closed Prison for Women. Soon after, she ran out of her daily medication and she still was not able to take her weekly medication. She wrote numerous petitions and letters with the inscription "Urgent" on top requesting an appointment with the prison infirmary doctor. She was not allowed up to the infirmary. About a month after her initial detention, she was taken to the Tarsus Public Hospital General Internal Medicine Department. She spoke to the doctor about her illness. She requested that all necessary bloodwork be carried out. However, she learned much later that they had only checked her hemogram, liver enzyme, TSH and ferritin numbers whereas the essential tests looking for the anti-DSDNA, C3, C4 and ANA numbers had not been worked up at all. Meanwhile, Mersin Anti-Terror Branch Office had lost the medical report about her illness. Later, she had seen her brother during a visitation and asked him to bring her medication and her medical report. Her brother brought them after one week. She couldn't use her medication for a total two-month time period.

– SLE is a condition in which the body's immune system is unable to recognize its own body tissue and starts attacking itself as though it were foreign matter. The body produces an excessive amount of antibodies (white blood cells) and the immune system starts slowly killing itself. This abnormality initially brings about a sudden drop in blood pressure, followed by joint pains, exhaustion, fatigue, and weakness to the point where a person is unable to sustain even basic functionality of life on their own. During the time period that she was in custody, she was only able to continue taking her daily medication. She was unable to take the treatment's main medication in a weekly and monthly basis. Eventually the disease relapsed. This disease can only be monitored and treated by a specialist rheumatology doctor. She needs to be under constant monitoring. The treatment of this illness requires specific procedures and is a critical process. Because there was no rheumatology department at Tarsus Public Hospital, she was constantly taken to the general medicine department. When she explained her situation to the doctor, the doctor said her illness could have relapsed and sent in a referral to the City Hospital rheumatology department. As of April 23, 2018, she was still not taken to the rheumatology department. Though she has been taking her medication after finally receiving it, she is not getting any better. She has had the disease of SLE for the last 15 years. Her illness is serious to the extreme and can certainly end in death. By her letter she files a grievance against all responsible persons in the Mersin Anti-Terror Branch Office, Tarsus Closed Prison for Women, and Tarsus Public Hospital, who have neglected and failed to act on their duties and responsibilities. (*Since the contents of the letters that Halime Gülsu wrote to the other institutions are the same, it is only the petition that she sent to the prosecutor's office which is summarized above.*)

G. FINDINGS

After our interviews, observations, and investigations we have found out the following:

1- In our investigation together with our physician members, Halime Gülsu's disease (SLE – Systemic Lupus Erythematosus) was determined to be fatal if not controlled using medication.

2- Considering the documents in the investigation file, the statement of Halime Gülsu's brother, the statement of the person who stayed with Halime Gülsu together both in the police custody and the prison ward, and the letters of Halime Gülsu which are consistent with the other documents, it is clear that that Halime Gülsu was detained for a long time, that she could not meet with her family during her detention, and some of her medications were not supplied in a timely manner.

3- She was arrested despite mentioning her illness in her statement she gave to the police and the prosecutor's office.

4- While she was in custody and then in prison, the treatment of SLE disease was not done. As a result, her illness progressed, the cause of her death was "cardiac arrest related to SLE."

5- Halime Gülsu was referred to the hospital repeatedly by the prison doctor. However, Tarsus State Hospital, which does not have a rheumatology service, referred her to the Mersin City Hospital only very late. Halime Gülsu was never admitted to the hospital.

RESULTS:

It is an indisputable fact that the right to life is the most fundamental human right accepted by all legal systems. The constitution of the Republic of Turkey obliges the government to take the necessary precautions and measures for the protection of human life.

In this context, since the medications of Halime Gülsu were not provided while she was in custody and then in prison, since she was arrested despite the fact that she had declared her illness during the investigation, and considering the fact that her treatment was not done properly or not at all, it appears that Halime Gülsu's death was due to negligence of the public authority, in particular due to "VIOLATION OF THE RIGHT TO LIFE" by the public authority.

In the case of Halime Gülsu, aside from the fault and negligence of the related persons, the ongoing issue is a system problem. It is clear that the legal, political, and social conjuncture supports and even compels the administrative and judicial authorities to act against the law.

Halime Gülsu is one of the many victims of the unjust treatment that the inmates are suffering from in the Turkish Prisons. The rights to life and health of the arrestees and convicts who are in similar situations must be protected. Especially the women and children in prisons, who are in similar situations, must be released. The necessary legislation must be enacted immediately.

Zeynep Kayadelen

Author Zeynep Kayadelen was born in Cankiri, Turkey on August 16, 1972. From the very early stages of her life, Kayadelen knew that she had to be involved in the magical world of words.

Even when she was only a toddler, she used to turn the pages of the books around and touch the letters to make some sense out of them.

When it was time, Kayadelen began attending elementary school with great enthusiasm and learned how to read and write so fast, just like a thirsty person who finally found water to drink.

She started to write regularly, pretty much from the day she learned how to read and write. She had somehow sensed during early childhood that life is only made up of some contents and ideas which could be expressed using words. She felt as if there were other magnificent worlds inside her, and the magic key to those worlds were words.

This was her driving motivation for reading and writing throughout her life. Kayadelen attended middle and high school at Sinop Teacher Training School. During this time period, she received awards in several poetry and prose contests. In 1989, Kayadelen got admitted to the Department of Teaching in Primary Education at Abant University, however she didn't complete her studies because she preferred to devote herself entirely to research and writing. During the time she spent in the university, she regularly wrote articles forthe college newspaper.

In her early career, she used to write more poetry. Later on, she mostly wrote novels and stories. Five of her novels have been published and printed in many editions in Turkey, namely Reyhan, Yitik Mevsim, Alpdoğan, Kadim Sır, and Menekşe Günler.

Kayadelen, enjoyed listening and writing tales because the intriguing atmosphere of the Eastern fairy tales had also rooted in her soul. As a result, she published two fairy tale books, Adsız

Oğlan ve Acayip Cüce (The nameless boy and the strange dwarf), and Örümcek Tüneli (The Spider Tunnel).

For a long time, Kayadelen has received education in screenwriting, and has worked in this field. She was one of the three screenwriters who wrote the script of the animation movie Allah'ın Sadık Kulu (Barla), which was released in 2011. The movie was the first in its genre for Turkey and had its place in the 50 highest-grossing Turkish movies of all time. Kayadelen wrote scripts for several TV series, too.

Kayadelen's main goal in life was to make this world a more peaceful and prosperous place, both for herself and others. That's why volunteer work and charity have become a way of life for her.

After the so-called coup attempt on July 15, 2016, groundless accusations were made against Kayadelen. Her name had been added. Escape from Turkey to the list of terrorists, among tens of thousands other innocent people. Her novels and story books had been banned and collected by the government. At the end, Kayadelen had to leave her belovedcountry without being able to take even one of her books.

After she escaped the darkness covering her homeland, she moved on to wherever she saw light and hope. Married with 5 children, she is now living in Toronto, Canada. While she continues to write about many different projects, Kayadelen also feels the responsibility to write about the ongoing tragedies in Turkey.

Kayadelen believes in the power of peace and love. In her view, what the world needs is more love and compassion, regardless of whatever it is that the people are fighting for.

Hafza Girdap is the executive director and the spokesperson for AST (Advocates of Silenced Turkey) and the founding member of Set ThemFree platform who works for the women's rights violated particularly in Turkey. Girdap is also a Ph.D. candidate in Women's and Gender Studies at Stony Brook University, New York. Girdap has a B.A. and M.A. in English Language and Literature. Her research areas are human rights and women's status in Muslim contexts, specifically the integration and adaptation of Muslim immigrant women while redefining their cultural identities. Girdap is interested in analyzing the lives of Muslim women regarding the challenges they face within their own cultures, before, during, and after conflicts. Her doctoral research focuses on self-identification and the gendered representation and reshaping of Muslim women who grew up in Islamic cultures but resettled to Western cultures. Her research takes an intersectional framework. In addition to her professional human rights work and academic studies, Girdap conducts researches at ECPS's gender program (European Center for Populism Studies https://www.populismstudies.org/about-us/

programs/gender/) as a nonresident research associate.

While carrying out her research, Girdap includes the voices of female survivors of conflict by examining the coping mechanisms used by these women to manage new and existing challenges, including social discrimination, oppression, violations of basic rights, etc. She studies how they manage when facing these challenges within different contexts, i.e. their own countries, refugee camps, and new settlements. Girdap has been living in the US since July 2016 as a result of political persecution she faced in her native Turkey. Since settling in the States, her research interests expanded and she has become much more involved in women's rights movements. Accordingly, she has participated in many programs and delivered speeches about the status of women in Muslim societies. Girdap has been organizing and speaking at UNGA and UN CSW panels for three years, with a focus on women's matters and experiences. She also mentors youth in the hope that they will become involved in these events as researchers and speakers. As having a personal motto in her life which is "Let Dreams Lead You!", Girdap is running online global bookclubs on Instagram where she also makes live interviews concerning women and youth empowerment. Hafza, with her two daughters (18 and 13 years) and her husband, is living on Long Island, New York.

AST PUBLISHING

Yarım
Kalan
Hikaye
Mina Leyla

The
Baby
in the
Bag
EDITED BY
HAFZA GİRDAP

Shoot me for
God's Sake
MINA LEILA

A PICTURE IS WORTH A THOUSAND WORDS:
THE ILLUSTRATIONS OF
A TEACHER IN PRISON
YOLGEZER

THE FAREWELL OF

Vefa
Diyarının
Sevdalıları
Şairlerden Seçme Şiirler

Zeynep Kayadelen
ESCAPE
FROM TURKEY
Edited by
Eyyup Esen

TÜRKİYE'Yİ
TERK EDENLER
Zeynep Kayadelen

True Stories of Oppression in Turkey
SILENT
SCREAM
Mina Leyla
Edited by:
Gunda Polat

AST PUBLISHING

IF YOU WOULD LIKE TO SUPPORT OUR BOOK PUBLISHING EFFORTS

https://silencedturkey.org/donatenow

PAYPAL
https://www.paypal.me/ast111

ZELLE
advocatesofsilencedturkey@gmail.com

PATREON
https://www.patreon.com/advocatesofsilencedturkey?alert=2

ADVOCATES OF SILENCED TURKEY

AST is a 501(c)(3) tax-exempt non-profit charitable and educational organization based in New Jersey, USA with the mission of defending human and civil rights.

EIN: 83-1568246

ADDRESS
Advocates of Silenced Turkey
P.O. Box 2399
Wayne, NJ 07474-2399

E-MAIL
help@silencedturkey.org

WEB & SOCIAL MEDIA
www.silencedturkey.org
twitter.com/silencedturkey
facebook.com/silencedturkey
youtube.com/advocatesofsilencedturkey